The collection of insightful essays
eschatology brings the Majority Worl
The church and the academy desper:
Western eschatologies have done both good and ill. This book notes that
reality, as well as the reality of major differences among various Christian
churches throughout the Majority World. Especially significant, however,
is the way these essays connect a robust Christian hope, and the biblical
eschatology that supports it, with present Christian existence and public
witness in particular cultures. Let us hope that these and other voices
continue to speak, and that this ending of a series is also a beginning –
the beginning of still more contextualized theologies and practices of hope,
especially where people and the rest of God's creation are suffering.

Michael J. Gorman, PhD
Raymond E. Brown Professor of Biblical Studies and Theology,
St Mary's Seminary & University, Baltimore, Maryland, USA

All too often eschatology is relegated to last chapters or to hurried summaries.
With this volume, Gene Green, Stephen Pardue, and K. K. Yeo offer us an
introduction to the expansive landscape of eschatologies in the Majority
World. This strong selection of essays helps us consider the rootedness of
oftentimes unexamined eschatologies in complex contexts. Wide-ranging in
location and in topic but grounded in specifics, each essay offers nuanced
reflection from Africa, Asia, and Latin America on concepts like death,
hope, and the kingdom of God. Each contributor challenges us to remember
that hope abstracted from the realities of colonization, imperialism, and
oppression is not true hope and reinforces how eschatology affects everything
from exegesis to ethics.

Amy Brown Hughes, PhD
Assistant Professor of Theology,
Gordon College, Wenham, Massachusetts, USA

Eschatology – the study of the end times – remains a fascinating and often
deeply contentious part of Christian theology. But as Christianity's center of
gravity moves ever more decisively outside the West, how does that affect
attitudes to themes from apocalyptic, to Zionism, to the nature of God's
kingdom? How are such ideas reinterpreted against the diverse cultural
and political backgrounds of Africa, Asia and Latin America? In a rich and
intriguing collection of essays by fine scholars, *All Things New* explores and
expounds ideas that have inspired thinkers since the earliest Christian ages.
A thoughtful and rewarding collection.

Philip Jenkins, PhD
Distinguished Professor of History,
Baylor University, Waco, Texas, USA

Like the rudder of a vessel, though less noticed, eschatology sets a direction for God's people (or *oikumene*) in diverse contexts. The unfolding of God's plan informs and guides today's church to faithfully bear witness to God's salvation. Thus, this book serves as the fitting conclusion and climax of this ground-breaking Majority World Theology Series.

Wonsuk Ma, PhD
Distinguished Professor of Global Christianity,
Oral Roberts University, Tulsa, Oklahoma, USA

Majority World Theology Series

Series Editors

Gene L. Green, Stephen T. Pardue, and K. K. Yeo

The Majority World Theology series exists because of the seismic shifts in the makeup of world Christianity. At this moment in history, more Christians live in the Majority World than in Europe and North America. However, most theological literature does not reflect the rising tide of Christian reflection coming from these regions. The Majority World authors in this series seek to produce, collaboratively, biblical and theological textbooks that are about, from, and to the Majority World. By assembling scholars from around the globe who share a concern to do theology in light of Christian Scripture and in dialogue with Christian tradition coming from the Western church, this series offers readers the chance to listen in on insightful, productive, and unprecedented in-person conversations. Each volume pursues a specific theological topic and is designed to be accessible to students and scholars alike.

Titles in This Series

Jesus without Borders: Christology in the Majority World
2015 | 9781783689170

The Trinity among the Nations: The Doctrine of God in the Majority World
2015 | 9781783681051

The Spirit over the Earth: Pneumatology in the Majority World
2016 | 978178368256

So Great a Salvation: Soteriology in the Majority World
2017 | 9781783683789

The Church from Every Tribe and Tongue: Ecclesiology in the Majority World
2018 | 9781783684489

All Things New: Eschatology in the Majority World
2019 | 9781783686469

All Things New

Eschatology in the Majority World

Edited by

Gene L. Green, Stephen T. Pardue, and K. K. Yeo

© 2019 Gene L. Green, Stephen T. Pardue, and K. K. Yeo

Published 2019 by Langham Global Library
An imprint of Langham Publishing
www.langhampublishing.org

Langham Publishing and its imprints are a ministry of Langham Partnership

Langham Partnership
PO Box 296, Carlisle, Cumbria, CA3 9WZ, UK
www.langham.org

ISBNs:
978-1-78368-646-9 Print
978-1-78368-724-4 ePub
978-1-78368-725-1 Mobi
978-1-78368-726-8 PDF

British Library Cataloguing-in-Publication Data
A catalogue record for this book is available from the British Library

ISBN: 978-1-78368-646-9

Cover art: © The Seven Trumpets by He Qi. www.heqiart.com
Cover & Book Design: projectluz.com

Contents

INTRODUCTION

STEPHEN T. PARDUE

In too many arrangements of systematic theology, eschatology functions much like an appendix, awkwardly affixed to the core of Christian teaching like an unnecessary limb. Even if it is unintentional, it is hard not to sense some deprioritizing when this part of Christian theology is called "last things," while matters such as prolegomena and revelation get to be called "first things," and the doctrine of God is called "theology proper." Regardless of titles, moreover, it is often the case that these doctrines bear examination only in the twilight of the theologian's attention, rather than in the bright dawn of God and the gospel.

This is a most unfortunate state of affairs, because there is a strong argument to be made that Jesus's teaching – and, indeed, the entire message of his life, death, and resurrection – cannot be rightly understood apart from eschatological commitments and claims. John the Baptist prepares the way for Jesus by proclaiming that "the kingdom of heaven has come near" (Matt 3:2 NIV) and by taking up Old Testament language clearly associated with the "Day of the Lord," a moment when Yahweh would intervene in the course of human events with finality, yielding judgment for those in rebellion against him, and perfect redemption for the people of Israel. Thus, the irony: far from being the subject of minor interest that it is now, eschatology was, in the very first declaration of the good news, a star player, a *sine qua non*.

In the twentieth century, several movements converged to bring eschatology back to the center of theological attention, each in a slightly different way. One of the most influential theologians of the twentieth century, Karl Barth, famously foregrounded eschatology, demanding that Christian theologians break with an increasingly prevalent habit of reducing Christian teaching to a set of ethical principles or philosophical ideals. Barth decried this tendency as a "de-eschatologization" of

Christianity,[1] and famously noted in the introduction to his commentary on Romans that "If Christianity be not altogether thoroughgoing eschatology, there remains in it no relationship whatever to Christ."[2] If theology is to be christological, in other words, it must also be intentionally eschatological through and through. Barth was hardly alone. As Richard Bauckham (himself a significant figure in twentieth-century eschatology) notes, Jürgen Moltmann brought a similar conviction to the project of modern theology, contending that "from first to last, and not merely in the epilogue, Christianity is eschatology."[3] To be sure, Barth, Moltmann, and other twentieth-century thinkers each had their own way of applying the eschatological turn, but all were convinced that eschatology must serve as the dominant interpretive lens through which Christian teaching must be refracted.

At least one key ingredient in this turn was emerging New Testament scholarship that sought to apply new tools and principles of historical scholarship to understanding the person of Jesus. In a rebuke to previous eras, figures like Albert Schweitzer and later Ernst Käsemann reminded scholars that their understanding of Jesus must not be disconnected from the cultural and political context in which Jesus emerged.[4] Viewed in this light, they contended, it is clear that Jesus is best understood as an eschatological prophet, and any interpretation of his life and work that misses this reality is ultimately pointing toward some formulated ideal rather than the authentic Jesus of Nazareth. While many aspects of the "quests" for the historical Jesus have been discarded, this insight has only gained surer footing in recent years, with a whole raft of new scholarship exploring the import of apocalyptic thought for understanding Jesus.[5]

---

1. Daniel L. Migliore, "Karl Barth's First Lectures in Dogmatics: Instruction in the Christian Religion," in Karl Barth, *The Göttingen Dogmatics: Instruction in the Christian Religion*, vol. 1, trans. Geoffrey W. Bromiley (Grand Rapids: Eerdmans, 1991), lviii.

2. Karl Barth, *The Epistle to the Romans*, trans. E. C. Hoskyns (Oxford: Oxford University Press, 1968), 314.

3. Jürgen Moltmann, *Theology of Hope*, trans. James W. Leitch (London: SCM, 1967), 16; quoted in Richard Bauckham, "Eschatology," in *The Oxford Handbook of Systematic Theology*, ed. John Webster, Kathryn Tanner, and Iain Torrance (Oxford: Oxford University Press, 2007), 306.

4. Bauckham, "Eschatology," 306–307.

5. For an introduction to this trend, see two compilations of essays in honor of a pioneering voice in this area, J. Louis Martyn: Marion L. Soards and Joel Marcus, eds., *Apocalyptic and the New Testament: Essays in Honor of J. Louis Martyn*, rev. ed. (London:

But eschatology also received a boost in the twentieth century from a less scholarly and more grassroots movement: the rise of dispensationalism. Rooted in the teachings of John Nelson Darby, dispensationalists pushed eschatology to the center of Christian consciousness through an emphasis on decoding biblical prophecies. Dispensationalist pastors and churchgoers spent much of the twentieth century conscientiously searching for connections between unfolding historical events – the rise of the Third Reich, the formation of the modern state of Israel, the dominance of the Soviet Union, to highlight a few examples – and biblical prophecies. Like Christians of all ages, they affirmed and looked forward to the return of Christ; what was new was the outsized attention given to the biblical teachings about the *parousia* and the events prophesied to precede it.[6]

Dispensationalist churches would gain an unlikely eschatological bedfellow in the latter half of the twentieth century: Pentecostal church movements. While Pentecostals differ markedly from dispensationalists in their assessment of the ongoing validity of particular spiritual gifts, they often share a similar commitment to a foregrounding of eschatology, affirming the imminent return of Christ, looking for the fulfillment of specific biblical prophecies in current world events, and seeing themselves as living "at the end of the age."[7]

Bloomsbury, 2015); and Joshua B. Davis and Douglas Karel Harink, eds., *Apocalyptic and the Future of Theology: With and Beyond J. Louis Martyn* (Eugene: Cascade, 2012).

6. Perhaps the best-known sensationalist account from this viewpoint was Hal Lindsey's *The Late Great Planet Earth* (Grand Rapids: Zondervan, 1970). However, readers should also note that many dispensationalist scholars, especially from the 1990s onward, sought an approach to the movement that maintained some of its core distinctives but was more circumspect with regard to its analysis of prophecy and contemporary events. See, e.g., Craig A. Blaising and Darrell L. Bock, *Progressive Dispensationalism* (Grand Rapids: BridgePoint, 1993); Craig L. Blomberg and Sung Wook Chung, eds., *A Case for Historic Premillennialism: An Alternative to "Left Behind" Eschatology* (Grand Rapids: Baker, 2009).

7. For an excellent introduction to distinctives of Pentecostal eschatologies, see Frank D. Macchia, "Pentecostal and Charismatic Theology," in *The Oxford Handbook of Eschatology*, ed. Jerry L. Walls (Oxford: Oxford University Press, 2007), 280–294; Peter Althouse and Robby Waddell, eds., *Perspectives in Pentecostal Eschatology: World without End* (Eugene: Wipf and Stock, 2010).

Eschatology and the Expansion of the Majority World Church

Coincidentally or not, the twentieth century turn toward all things eschatological occurred at almost exactly the same time as an explosion of growth in the Majority World church. As each of these movements advanced the eschatological agenda in different ways, remarkable church expansion was being activated in Asia, Africa, and Latin America. While the beginning of the twentieth century saw only a small fraction of the world's Christians living outside of the West, by the turn of the millennium Christians living outside the West were the clear majority. A specific case can help drive home the significance of this broad claim: consider that in spite of decades of persecution and marginalization, Christians in China now outnumber those in the United Kingdom, which was one of the major centers of the world Christian movement throughout the nineteenth and early twentieth centuries.

In many cases, these Majority World expansions were directly linked to eschatological thinking. In Latin America, for example, theologies that emphasized the establishment of the kingdom and the hope that it offered to the poor and oppressed were instrumental in revitalizing the church and equipping it for ongoing mission. In other cases, there is strong evidence that mission activity in the Majority World was driven primarily by a sense that the church must redeem the brief time left before the second coming, or even that through the making disciples of all nations, the church may be able to hasten the second coming.[8] To return to the contemporary Chinese church, a prominent example of eschatology's ongoing influence in mission is the Back to Jerusalem movement, a loosely organized campaign that sees churches in China supplying an enormous missionary workforce in the years ahead to penetrate the unevangelized nations between China and the Holy Land. The vision of the movement is rooted in a set of very specific convictions about the eschaton: especially that China has been providentially blessed at this specific moment in time, and "that God has given [us] a solemn responsibility to take the fire from his altar and complete the Great Commission by establishing God's Kingdom in all of the remaining countries and people groups in Asia,

8. Craig Ott, Stephen J. Strauss, and Timothy C. Tennent, *Encountering Theology of Mission: Biblical Foundations, Historical Developments, and Contemporary Issues*, Encountering Mission (Grand Rapids: Baker, 2010), 186–191.

the Middle East, and Islamic North Africa."[9] The movement explicitly affirms a premillennial eschatology, and, in many cases, includes an affinity for political Israel.[10]

And so we are confronted in the twentieth century with two coinciding trends: what we might call the "re-eschatologization" of Christian theology, and the shift of the church's primary center of gravity to the Majority World. At first glance, the two developments seem to be of a piece: at the same time that professional Christian theologians were rediscovering the centrality of eschatology for Christian teaching, Christian practitioners had the same thought. Both parties helped propagate a renewed vision for eschatology in their own way – with professional theologians influencing the academic literature on the one hand, and church practitioners influencing in-the-trenches ministry on the other.

But a closer look reveals a far more complicated picture. For example, it is notable that some of these movements have been quite at odds in terms of how Christian eschatology should influence Christian life. At least in certain forms, dispensationalist and Pentecostal theologies often perceive Christian eschatological teaching to have a primarily extractive force: because the world is not my home, and because we are so near to the end of all things, our limited resources are best focused on evangelism and the building up of the church, not on the transformation of this-worldly realities through civic engagement or ecological care.[11] In contrast, theologians like N. T. Wright and J. Richard Middleton have spilled much ink arguing precisely the opposite: namely, that biblical eschatology should push Christians to greater engagement with this-

---

9. Quoted from backtojerusalem.com in Tobias Brandner, "Mission, Millennium, and Politics: A Continuation of the History of Salvation – from the East," *Missiology: An International Review* 37, no. 3 (2009): 319.

10. Brandner, "Mission, Millennium, and Politics," 327–328. See Shirley Ho's essay in this volume for a fascinating examination of how these pro-Israel beliefs have influenced the church in Taiwan.

11. Many will no doubt identify with James K. A. Smith's description of the evangelical eschatology with which he was initially brought to faith: "It was very much a rapture-ready, heaven-centric piety that had little, if anything, to say about how or why a Christian might care about urban planning or chemical engineering or securing clean water sources in developing nations. Why worry about justice or flourishing in a world that is going to burn up?" (James K. A. Smith, *Awaiting the King: Reforming Public Theology* [Grand Rapids: Baker, 2017], 85).

worldly realities in light of God's desire to renew all things through the church's ministry of reconciliation.[12]

Another complication in the narrative relates to the influence of eschatology in the thought of Christians in the Majority World. As the essays in this volume make clear, eschatology has significantly shaped the dynamics and self-understanding of Christians in the Majority World. And yet, as William Dryness and Oscar García-Johnson have recently noted, there are "relatively few works that specifically address eschatology outside the West."[13] Specifically, Dyrness and García-Johnson are concerned by the paucity of contextualized reflections on eschatology in the Majority World, "especially in Africa and Asia," where "Western eschatology had a great, and not always positive, influence."[14] If eschatology gained such centrality in Christian theology at just the time that Majority World churches have been expanding, why the shortage of contextually rooted eschatological theologies?

Plan of the Book

These are just some of the complications that the present volume is uniquely positioned to expose, wrestle with, and begin untangling. D. Stephen Long begins the discussion with an insightful examination of the ongoing value of first-century apocalyptic as a resource for contemporary Christian eschatology. After offering a detailed account of the recovery of apocalyptic thought in recent scholarship, he engages with a series of objections to its influence in Christian eschatology. While it is certainly the case that irresponsible interpretations of apocalyptic literature can veer into dangerous territory, Long contends that ridding Christian eschatology of its apocalyptic underpinnings is a fool's errand. Rather than *less* apocalyptic imagination, the global church desperately needs a *deeper* and *richer* vision of the apocalyptic: one that unveils not only the culminating judgment that awaits the world, but also the vision of God dwelling with his people in a new heaven and new earth.

12. N. T. Wright, *Surprised by Hope: Rethinking Heaven, the Resurrection, and the Mission of the Church* (New York: HarperOne, 2014); J. Richard Middleton, *New Heaven and a New Earth: Reclaiming Biblical Eschatology* (Grand Rapids: Baker Academic, 2014).

13. William A. Dyrness and Oscar García-Johnson, *Theology without Borders: An Introduction to Global Conversations* (Grand Rapids: Baker Academic, 2015), 140.

14. Dyrness and García-Johnson, *Theology without Borders*, 140.

Long's essay explores well the tension with which many of the book's remaining essays wrestle: namely, that between recognizing the future orientation of the Christian faith and the pressing needs confronting the church in the here and now. This theme is echoed in the two succeeding essays from James Kombo and John Ekem. Kombo starts by offering a fascinating survey of eschatology in African Christian thought. He notes that African Christians approach eschatology not only in cosmic terms – that is, as a consideration of how all things will be restored or reconciled in Christ – but also in very personal terms. In particular, he draws attention to the discussion of what has been termed "the intermediate state," the time between bodily death and bodily resurrection. While this "in-between" time has often been ignored or minimized in Western eschatologies, the African context, with its emphasis on the ongoing life of the ancestors, requires that we articulate how God provides for and governs this phase of life after death. He argues persuasively that Christian theology has internal resources to respond well to these questions, and that, in the process, African theological reflection can help Western eschatology be refined and enriched.

If Kombo creates a framework for such enrichment, Ekem provides a concrete example of it. Like Long, Ekem reminds readers that the strange and sometimes unsettling world of apocalyptic literature is an unavoidable feature of Christian eschatology – it is the language that Jesus chooses to use when asked about the end of all things, and it is also the genre through which Revelation communicates the most comprehensive Christian vision of the end. Ekem specifically examines Revelation 21's vision of the new heaven and new earth, considering how the original author's vision translates and communicates in the contemporary Ghanaian context. The results of his analysis are fascinating. The Ghanaian context reveals shades of nuance and emphasis in Revelation 21 that are easily lost in contemporary English translations, and the African worldview that Kombo so ably described prompts new and interesting questions about the nature of the text and its impact on Christian thought.

The next two essays in the book once again bring together the insights of a systematic theologian and a biblical scholar, this time exploring the dynamics of Christian eschatology in Latin America. Alberto Roldán offers a broad survey of the landscape of eschatology in Latin American contexts, focusing especially on the contrast between dispensationalist eschatology that dominated in the decades after World War II, and the much broader eschatological visions that gained influence in the later part of the twentieth century. Roldán argues that these eschatological movements, especially those that echo Moltmann's insights in *Theology of Hope*, have much to offer the contemporary evangelical church, as they often strike impressive balances between the promise of future salvation and the Christian commitment to here-and-now transformation. He concludes the essay by showing how this plays out in the real world, noting how Christian hymnody tells a particular eschatological story that rightly shapes the posture and perspective of churchgoers.

Nelson Morales is likewise interested in the real-world implications of eschatological teaching, but examines instead the diverse interpretations in Latin American churches of Jesus's famous announcement recorded in Mark 1:15: "The time has come . . . The kingdom of God has come near" (NIV). Understanding how various networks within the Latin American church have heard and interpreted this declaration turns out to be a potent heuristic for understanding the implications of various eschatological views. Ultimately, Morales argues that evangelicals in Latin America would be wise to make the most of these insights by recognizing both the future fulfillment and the present unfolding of the kingdom in our present world.

The final two essays in the book, from Aldrin Peñamora and Shirley Ho, offer a glimpse of how the church in Asia – a minority nestled in a continent where the major world religions all find their home – understands and articulates the uniquely Christian vision of the end. Peñamora examines four influential movements in Asia, and considers how their unusual – and remarkably effective – ministries each depended upon a profoundly eschatological vision. Each case study offers a unique insight into how Asian believers have approached the doctrine of eschatology, even as they experience extreme forms of success and blessing (e.g. in the case of David Yonggi Cho's ministry in Korea) and suffering (e.g. Watchman Nee's experience in China). Peñamora argues that while we should be grateful that Christian theology has the diverse resources to speak to the broad array of experiences present in Asia, the Asian church must be especially attentive to the gospel's clarion call to stand alongside the suffering, marginalized, and downtrodden.

Finally, Shirley Ho's essay assesses the eschatological underpinnings of the Zionist movement in Taiwan. Ho is not only an able tour guide – offering readers a remarkable glimpse into a world in which rams' horns are blown, traditional Jewish clothing is worn, and Jewish festivals are celebrated thousands of miles and worlds away from Israel – but more importantly helps to explain the rationale and worldview underlying these practices. After noting how Taiwanese Christians within this movement read a key text about the restoration of Israel, Ho offers her own reading, which artfully connects the world of the original author and audience with Taiwanese history and culture. Using the concept of harmony (*Ta-tung*), she ably narrates a more robust vision of eschatology that is biblically rooted and also contextually formed.

For theology to be eschatological is to acknowledge that the gospel is first and foremost an announcement of good news about God's redemptive kingdom and plan. The fact that this good news is for every people in every culture and place has classically led Christians to affirm that its unpacking is best accomplished with the whole church, allowing the fullness of truth to shine through our diverse cultural identities. This is what it means for theology to be catholic, and it is the fundamental affirmation underlying the Majority World Theology series. It is a great joy to see these two truths come together in this book – that is, not only to see eschatology recognized as a central aspect of all Christian theology, but also to see it assessed in a context of true catholicity. It is our hope that the book will therefore serve as a unique aid to the church in its journey of seeking to apprehend, submit to, and live out the good eschatological news among every tribe, nation, people, and tongue.

Compiling a book like this is impossible without a team of remarkable people working together. Of course, first on this list are the authors and their respective institutions, for making the time for this project in the midst of their many and varied commitments. They are our heroes. We are also grateful for the steady help of ScholarLeaders in standing behind and beside us as we have developed the Majority World Theology series, and no less so in this case. Larry Smith, Evan Hunter, and Lynn Simons deserve our thanks for seeing the strategic value of the series from the start. They provided crucial assistance in securing resources and managing logistics to enable scholars from four continents to gather in Boston in November 2017. Without that gathering, the book would not have been possible. We owe a deep debt to Langham Publishing, and especially to Pieter Kwant, Luke Lewis, and Vivian Doub, for their unwavering commitment and assistance in the publication of this book and all the others in the series. In addition, we wish to thank Suzanne Mitchell for her editorial assistance, and Jixun Hu for his work on the indices. Finally, of course, we give thanks for the Lord's faithfulness in bringing this project to fruition. All glory to him who was, and is, and is to come.

CHAPTER 1

Eschatology, Apocalyptic, Ethics, and Political Theology

D. STEPHEN LONG

ABSTRACT

This essay first examines the perceived failures of apocalyptic in modernity: it is other-worldly, foments an extreme, violent politics, or produces a political Zionism that destabilizes the international political order. For this reason, some theologians divide eschatology from apocalyptic, but this is an unsustainable division. If there were no apocalyptic literature, there would be no eschatology. The key question is how to interpret apocalyptic literature for eschatology. The conclusion offers a theological interpretation of the Apocalypse.

Introduction

Eschatology is the doctrine of the end times or ultimate things. Eschatology comes from the Greek work *eschaton*, which means "last." It contains many important themes. Here are six of the most important: (1) the restoration of Israel; (2) the coming of the kingdom or reign of God; (3) the renewal of creation; (4) heaven and earth, God's dwelling place and the creaturely dwelling place, coming together in unity; (5) final judgment; (6) the completion, fulfillment, or perfection of history.

These themes are present in the Nicene Creed, the most universally used expression of faith among Christians throughout the world. Many recite it weekly, confessing the following words about Jesus:

For our sake he was crucified under Pontius Pilate,

> he suffered death and was buried,
> and rose again on the third day
> in accordance with the Scriptures.
> He ascended into heaven
> and is seated at the right hand of the Father.
> He will come again in glory
> to judge the living and the dead
> and his kingdom will have no end.

Here is the basic confession of Christian eschatology. Through his death and resurrection, Jesus has been enthroned as Ruler of the world. His reign will be one of divine glory. Every Christian worship service is a repetition of Jesus's enthronement as Ruler, but it is also a recognition that, as Hebrews 2:8 states, everything is not yet subject to his reign. For this reason, Christians also regularly confess, "Christ is come. Christ has died. Christ will come again." The expectation of his coming anticipates judgment. Although injustice, inequality, hatred, and violence seem to have the last word, no one can finally escape her or his wrongdoings. They must be accounted for. But the judgment is not to condemn; it brings life – his reign will have no end, and unlike other reigns it will not be based upon deception and violence. The petition from the Lord's Prayer, "thy kingdom come, thy will be done, on earth as it is in heaven," expresses this eschatological hope.

The above brief exposition of eschatology presents a Christian eschatology. However, eschatology does not need to be religious; it can also be secular. Reinhold Niebuhr interpreted that period of Western history known as the Renaissance with its emphasis on progress as one side of the development of Christian eschatology. The other side, the Reformation, developed the pessimistic. The former focused on renewal; the latter on judgment.[1] Many thinkers have suggested that Karl Marx's view of a communist society bears strong similarities to Jewish and Christian eschatology. Some have called it a secularized eschatology. Marx sees a dialectic that runs through history moving us toward that stage when, rather than laboring away at a single vocation, everyone engages in various tasks without those tasks becoming their identity: "hunt in the morning, fish in the afternoon, rear cattle in the evening,

---

1. Reinhold Niebuhr, *The Nature and Destiny of Man*, vol. 2 (New York: Charles Scribner's Sons, 1964), 156–169.

criticize after dinner, just as I have a mind, without ever becoming hunter, fisherman, shepherd or critic."[2]

While Marx's thought as a secularized eschatology has been suggested by many, fewer seem to have noticed that Adam Smith's *Wealth of Nations* takes its title from a Jewish and Christian eschatological passage, Isaiah 60:5. Isaiah tells the people of Israel what will happen when they return to Jerusalem after exile:

> Lift up your eyes and look around;
> they all gather together, they come to you;
> your sons shall come from far away,
> and your daughters shall be carried on their nurses' arms.
> Then you shall see and be radiant;
> your heart shall thrill and rejoice,
> because the abundance of the sea shall be brought to you,
> the wealth of the nations shall come to you.

Another source for secular eschatology is technology when it is assumed that it can deliver what Christian faith hoped for, but never delivered: life without end, a promise set forth in some post-human evolution in which humans merge with technology to create everlasting life.

The above Jewish, Christian, and secular views of eschatology all assume that something is being restored, which also means that something needs restoration. Everything is not as it should be. To see the world as it is and realize that it should not be is the first step in eschatology. The next step is to see the world as it should be coming into existence – lions lie down with lambs, the hungry are fed, pain and suffering no longer exist, justice is done, and wrongs are righted. Eschatology, then, is a teaching about judgment and restoration. It can have a secular goal that suggests that if we follow these economic or political principles, injustices will be overcome and the wealth of nations will come to all. It can have a religious goal. Eschatology is the renewal and restoration of Israel, the church, or of all creation. Its influence in Western society is pervasive, both in secular and religious forms. Yet Western thinkers, religious and secular, have also been concerned that the influence of Jewish and Christian eschatology has had detrimental political and ethical consequences.

---

2. From Marx's *Economic and Philosophical Manuscripts*, in Eric Fromm, *Marx's Concept of Man*, trans. T. B. Bottomore (New York: Unger, 1986), 206.

D. *Stephen Long*

The following essay begins with secular and religious thinkers who express grave reservations about eschatology's influence. It then moves to discuss a pervasive feature of Western eschatology that has had, and continues to have, global political repercussions: Zionism, old and new. As other chapters in this work ably demonstrate, the emphasis on a Christian Zionism has had marked global influence. The essay then examines different readings of eschatology, ethics, and politics among diverse contemporary Western thinkers that do not require Christian Zionism. It concludes by suggesting that the most constructive way forward for Christian eschatology is its cultivation of an apocalyptic imagination that arises from a fullness of worship and that is repeatedly relevant for a theopolitical vision.

Perceived Failures of Apocalyptic

Because it assumes that the world as it is should not be, eschatology can be dangerous. It looks for something other than what exists, and that could motivate persons to wish for the destruction of what is for the sake of what is coming. Several Western thinkers expressed grave concern about eschatology. In the nineteenth century, the philosopher Friedrich Nietzsche announced the "twilight of the idols." By "idols" he meant theological ideas like God, the church, and eschatology. He imagined that by our generation these theological ideas would no longer hold people captive. The contemporary political philosopher Mark Lilla announces and laments that "the twilight of the idols has been postponed." Lilla finds it "incomprehensible" that apocalyptic or eschatological ideas are still with us and continue to inform politics, much to its detriment. He writes, "We are disturbed and confused. We find it incomprehensible that theological ideas still inflame the minds of men, stirring up messianic passions that leave societies in ruin. We assumed that this was no longer possible, that human beings had learned to separate religious questions from political ones, that fanaticism was dead. We were wrong."[3] Notice that he correlates "messianic passions" with fanaticism. To hope for a messiah, to think one knows who the messiah is and how he is coming, suggests Lilla, inflames fanatics who

---

3. Mark Lilla, *The Stillborn God: Religion, Politics and the Modern West* (New York: Knopf, 2007), 3.

seek to destroy political societies as they currently exist for the sake of the messianic society that is arriving. Lilla characterizes apocalyptic as focusing on revelation. Apocalyptic denies that knowledge of God moves from humanity to God. In contrast, it emphasizes God's unpredictable in-breaking, relativizing the present and political structures. Apocalyptic is catastrophic. It looks for the destruction of the world.

Lilla is not alone in lamenting the ongoing influence of apocalyptic; there is a long tradition of Western philosophers who rejected eschatology because of its political and ethical consequences. Immanuel Kant (1724–1804) was an influential philosopher who focused on how it is that we can come to know what we know. He was less concerned about what eschatology did to politics than about what it did to philosophy. In 1796, he wrote an essay entitled "On a Newly Arisen Superior Tone of Philosophy." The "superior tone" arose from religious enthusiasts who thought that they had a mystical vision that gave them certain knowledge. These enthusiasts, he suggested, reduced philosophy to a "mode whereby secrets are revealed."[4] Apocalyptic, he thought, is the unveiling of secrets so that once philosophy took this apocalyptic tone, it "must necessarily promise a surrogate of cognition, supernatural communication (mystical illumination), which is the death of all philosophy."[5] Anyone who thinks that he or she has a secure source of knowledge from supernatural communication will no longer engage in critical thinking. They will be led by a misguided vision.

G. W. F. Hegel (1770–1831) wrote after Kant and, like him, emphasized political freedom. He also claimed that "otherworldly eschatology is the enemy of political and economic freedom."[6] If you found your true home in the eschaton, you would not work for the political and economic freedom available to finite human creatures in the here and now. Karl Marx (1818–1883) agreed and developed Hegel's idea in a more critical political and economic vein. Eschatology promised poor workers that even though they were suffering now and not yet receiving their reward, they would be rewarded when they entered the kingdom of God at the end of life. Eschatology was oppressive because it masked

---

4. I. Kant, "On a Newly Arisen Superior Tone in Philosophy," in *Raising the Tone of Philosophy: Late Essay by Immanuel Kant, Transformative Critique by Jacques Derrida*, ed. Peter Fenves (Baltimore and London: Johns Hopkins University Press, 1993), 51.

5. Kant, "On a Newly Arisen Superior Tone in Philosophy," 62.

6. Cited in Luke Bretherton, *Resurrecting Democracy: Faith, Citizenship, and the Politics of a Common Life* (New York: Cambridge University Press, 2015), 227.

the alienation workers should recognize between their labor and its just reward. Eschatology was used by the powerful to sedate the poor and provide false comfort to the sufferings of the exploited.

Kant, Hegel, and Marx were not alone. From the eighteenth century until today, influential Western philosophers have expressed grave reservations about apocalyptic thinking due to its perceived detrimental effects. It causes people to flee from the world or even hate it, hoping for its destruction. Few of these critics have been as strident as the atheist Christopher Hitchens. He accused religion of being "violent, irrational, intolerant, allied to racism and tribalism, invested in ignorance and hostile to free inquiry." He added to this the charge that it "looks forward to the destruction of the world."[7] Here, too, apocalyptic is the reason for religious violence because apocalyptic envisions a catastrophic end to the world in which everything is destroyed in a great conflagration. These concerns are not unwarranted. In the sixteenth century, especially in Münster, Germany, Christians known as the radical wing of the Reformation thought that the end of the world was coming and the result was violence perpetrated by them and against them. In 1978, when an apocalyptic sect known as Jonestown committed mass suicide, 909 people died. In 1993, an apocalyptic sect known as the Branch Davidians thought along similar lines and the result was violence perpetrated by them and against them. Given these sentiments about the dangers of apocalyptic, and the historical events that seem to corroborate them, many Christians have been wary of embracing the doctrine of eschatology.

Zionism: New and Old

The controversies swirling around various types of Zionism accentuate the concerns of many Western philosophers and theologians about eschatology. Jewish Zionism was a movement in the latter part of the nineteenth century to provide a homeland for Jews in Israel, including a state. Christian Zionism differs. It is an eschatologically charged political movement that seeks to create political conditions that would lead to the second coming of Jesus. In its fundamentalist, dispensationalist

---

7. Christopher Hitchens, *God Is Not Great: How Religion Poisons Everything* (New York: Twelve, Hatchette Book Group, 2007), 56.

form, Christian Zionism views eschatology as a decoded map, by which we can discern or even encourage the development of conditions that allow Israel's political development to pave the way for Jesus's second coming. This popular movement has little backing among New Testament scholars and theologians. However, one common theme running through the essays in this book is how pervasive something like Christian Zionism is throughout global Christianity. Shirley Ho traces its importance and influence in Taiwan. Alberto Roldán demonstrates the influence of dispensationalist eschatology in Latin American Protestantism, even as he points to movements in Latin America that are now moving away from dispensationalism. Nelson Morales presents an eschatology that is an alternative to this Christian Zionism. The kingdom of God is not the restoration of the "land of Israel," but "a new order inaugurated by Jesus" that can be established wherever his disciples are faithful. James Kombo presents it in terms of an African ontology.

These diverse accounts of eschatology raise the question: What is being restored? Is it a literal return of Jews to Israel, and the rebuilding of the temple? A "new" articulation of Christian Zionism argues that eschatology must include not only the land of, but also the state of Israel. Gerald R. McDermott represents the new Christian Zionism, stating, "We believe that the return of Jews to the land and their establishment of the state of Israel are partial fulfillments of biblical prophecy and so are part of God's design for what might be a long era of eschatological fulfillment. As Mark Kinzer puts it, today's state of Israel both awaits redemption and is a means to it. It is a proleptic sign of the eschaton, which means that it is a provisional sign of the not-yet-actualized consummation."[8] McDermott distances the "new" Christian Zionism from that found among fundamentalist dispensationalists, who put "Israel and the church on two different tracks," have an "elaborated schedule of end-time events," and view Christians as raptured while Jews and others are lost.[9] The "new" Christian Zionism does not have these convictions, although it does wed biblical prophecy to a defense of the state of Israel.

Nicholas R. Brown asks what Jesus has restored in his strange victory, and makes a biblical argument that the land of Israel must be in-

---

8. Gerald R. McDermott, "Introduction: What Is the New Christian Zionism?," in *The New Christian Zionism*, ed. Gerald R. McDermott (Downers Grove: InterVarsity Press, 2016), 14.

9. McDermott, "Introduction," 11.

cluded in any eschatological vision. He dissects contemporary eschatologies and suggests that they lose the importance of land through three different strategies: "praxification, ecclesiofication and typofication." The first turns the restoration of the land of Israel into an ethical praxis. Wherever this ethical praxis can be found, eschatological restoration has begun. The second views the church as sufficient for restoration. When Jesus claimed that he will destroy the temple and rebuild it, the biblical writers identified his body as the site for restoration. The land is no longer necessary because we have the church as the continuation of Christ's body. The third views the restoration as a political type that can become the pattern for any nation state.[10] Although Brown agrees in part with these three views, he argues that each of them loses the importance of the land. The land and Jesus's prophetic proclamation of God's reign must be held together. While the three views noted above lose the "connection" of the land to the kingdom, the "Christian Zionists . . . tend to detach that connection from Jesus' proclamation of the kingdom."[11] They lose his prophetic critique.

What is restored in Christian eschatology? From the above discussion on Zionism new and old, it is at least evident that this restoration has political and ethical consequences. The next section examines a different account of eschatology and its relation to those consequences.

Eschatology, Apocalyptic, Ethics, and Politics

If it were not for a genre of Jewish and Christian literature known as apocalyptic, there would be no eschatology. Examples of apocalyptic literature can be found in the book of Daniel in the Old Testament and Revelation in the New Testament. The Greek word for Revelation is *Apokalypsis*, from which we get the term "apocalypse." Christian theology has a doctrine of eschatology because of apocalyptic literature. As I noted in the first section above, apocalyptic literature became controversial in the West after the seventeenth century. For a long time, theologians ignored eschatology and apocalyptic by emphasiz-

10. Nicholas Brown identifies Glenn Stassen and David Gushee with the first approach, Stanley Hauerwas and John Howard Yoder with the second, and Oliver O'Donovan with the third. See Nicholas Brown, *For the Nation: Jesus, the Restoration of Israel and Articulating a Christian Ethic of Territorial Governance* (Eugene: Pickwick, 2016), 65–83.

11. Brown, *For the Nation*, 192.

ing Jesus as an ethical teacher who taught about the kingdom of God, something that could be brought about by human effort. In one sense, the popular Christian Zionism of fundamentalist dispensationalism filled the gap this abandonment of eschatology left in more mainline Christian thought.

The German biblical scholar and theologian Albert Schweitzer (1875–1965) challenged any understanding of Jesus that could adopt his ethics and abandon his eschatology. Schweitzer argued that the historical Jesus could not be rightly understood apart from his eschatology. However, Schweitzer thought that no modern person could affirm Jesus's eschatology, so the relevance of Jesus for modern times would have to lie elsewhere than in his historical and eschatological context. Since Schweitzer's work, theologians have recognized the importance of Jesus's eschatology for understanding him, but they have responded to it differently. Some have dismissed that context, replacing it with something else, such as the command to love God, neighbors, and enemies. Others have affirmed it, but distinguish eschatology from apocalyptic, treating the former as a more general discipline and the latter as a problem to be overcome because of its perceived specificity. Still others do not divide eschatology and apocalyptic and suggest that Christian ethics cannot be understood without apocalyptic.

Schweitzer's Retrieval of Apocalyptic

One way to avoid apocalyptic was to disregard any sense that Jesus was an apocalyptic thinker. Western biblical scholars and theologians did this by emphasizing Jesus's proclamation of the "kingdom of God," but they did so in such a way that the reign of God he announces is not something that interrupts the world as it is; it is not an in-breaking, but it gradually emerges over time from his ethical teachings. The ethical teachings that were proposed looked much like the dominant ethics of Western, European society. In this tradition of thought, Jesus does not challenge politics as it is, but perpetuates it. He gives us resources to do what is already being done, fostering a civilization of democracy and freedom. The difficulty with this tradition of thought, as Schweitzer pointed out, is that it read itself into the historical Jesus and neglected his radical, apocalyptic thinking. After Schweitzer's work, that tradition could no longer consider itself to be putting forth the historical

Jesus. Once Jesus became an apocalyptic prophet, it was not so easy to remake him into the image of a respectable, democratic, Western man.

Schweitzer challenged the liberal interpretation of Jesus that reduced his work to modern ethics by convincingly demonstrating that Jesus's mission could only be understood in his apocalyptic context. Jesus did not expect human beings to create the kingdom of God; it would come about by an in-breaking from God into creaturely existence that Jesus thought was imminent. For that reason, Schweitzer stated, the Jesus who preached the "ethic of the Kingdom of God never had any existence. He is a figure designed by rationalism, endowed with life by liberalism and clothed by modern theology in an historical garb."[12] Because he thought the kingdom of God was about to arrive, he could "throw himself on the wheel of history," sacrificing everything – family, property, relationships, power. God was bringing something completely new so everything that existed prior to it could be jettisoned. For Schweitzer, eschatology and ethics were contraries. He writes, "There is for Jesus no ethic of the Kingdom of God, for in the Kingdom of God all natural relationships, even for example the distinction of sex, are abolished."[13] Jesus was an apocalyptic prophet who imagined that the end times were about to interrupt human history, but he was wrong. Jesus did not stop history when he threw himself upon the "wheel of history"; it grinded on, destroying eschatological expectation. Jesus's failure as an apocalyptic prophet meant that no one could take those expectations seriously. Thus, rather than creating the conditions for the eschaton, "he has destroyed them."[14]

Ethics in Place of Eschatology

Schweitzer's work on Jesus's apocalypticism accomplished two things in Western theology. First, apocalyptic returned as a necessary context in which to understand Jesus. Second, apocalyptic was largely considered indefensible. Jesus's mission was inextricably linked with his eschatology, but, because the latter was unacceptable to modern persons, something must replace eschatology if Jesus was to be conceived as relevant.

12. Albert Schweitzer, *The Quest of the Historical Jesus: A Critical Study of Its Progress from Reimarus to Wrede* (Baltimore: Johns Hopkins Press, 1998), 398.
13. Schweitzer, *Quest*, 365.
14. Schweitzer, 371.

Often, what replaced eschatology was ethics. Take as an example the influential work of Paul Ramsey in his 1950 *Basic Christian Ethics*. He identified *agape* or disinterested love as the heart of Jesus's teaching and he too connected it with eschatology. When Jesus tells us to do something difficult like love our enemy, give everything to the poor, or resist calling someone a fool, his "strenuous" sayings depend "on his apocalyptic expectation." Agreeing with the American theologian Walter Rauschenbusch (1861–1918), Ramsey argued that Jesus's apocalyptic context is untenable for moderns. We can neither "translate" his love commands from that apocalyptic context without significant loss, nor can we inhabit it. We are caught in a conundrum. Jesus's ethics arise from apocalyptic expectation, but modern, reasonable people cannot inhabit Jesus's eschatological world. What is to be done? Ramsey argued that Jesus's teaching could still have "validity" without the eschatology. The "genesis" of the love commandment in its apocalyptic context had "nothing to do with validity."[15] What Jesus teaches can be differentiated from how he taught it and still function as a Christian ethics. Ethics can be divided from eschatology.

Eschatology as Necessary for Ethics

This longstanding modern division between ethics and eschatology was unstable. Later in his work, Ramsey qualified his earlier statements about eschatology and affirmed its importance for Christian ethics. In so doing, he was following some mid-twentieth-century theological shifts, largely brought about by the Swiss Protestant theologian Karl Barth (1886–1968) and the Swiss Roman Catholic theologian Hans Urs von Balthasar (1905–1988). They retrieved eschatology and made it central to their theology.

Barth wrote a famous essay in 1922 in which he stated that the supposed certainties of Western ethics had become more of a problem than Christian dogma. Ethics could no longer substitute for Christian doctrine. Rather than ethics substituting for eschatology, ethics is intelligible within eschatology. In his famous *Commentary on the Epistle to the Romans* (1922), he stated, "Thus it is that all these human possibilities be-

---

15. Paul Ramsey, *Basic Christian Ethics* (Louisville: Westminster/John Knox Press, 1993) 36, 41.

come ethical only in the shadow of the final eschatological possibility."[16] The human possibilities are generosity, mercy, and cheerfulness, especially as they bring a new conception of authority. To bring about this new conception, the human person must be "disturbed." Eschatology disturbs human nature, interrupting and even contradicting it to bring something new.

Fifteen years after Barth's Romans commentary, Balthasar published a three-volume work entitled "Apocalypse of the German Soul."[17] Apocalyptic had never disappeared from Germany, he suggested, but it was negatively present. It often functioned in German literature as the emptying out of God into humanity. The basic teaching of the incarnation that God became human had become a strict passage from the divine to the human. What had been considered divine had become nothing but human. Barth was the only theologian Balthasar cited in his three-volume work; Barth offers a different understanding of eschatology. There was much to appreciate in Barth, but his early work was too dialectical for Balthasar. By that he meant that God was only present to humanity as a negation of what it meant to be human. Balthasar also affirmed apocalyptic, but he did so analogically. The eschaton does not simply negate what comes before, but preserves and perfects what is true, good, and beautiful in creation. Balthasar thought that Barth's later work moved away from dialectic to analogy and thus provided us with a better understanding of apocalyptic and its relation to creation.

An Eschatological Ethics: The Church and the Two Ages

After Barth and Balthasar, apocalyptic has continued to hold an important place for many Christian theologians and ethicists. Three American theologians – John Howard Yoder, William James McClendon, and Stanley Hauerwas – and one British theologian – Oliver O'Donovan – have argued that Christian ethics makes no sense without eschatology. Yoder, McClendon, and Hauerwas draw on eschatology for a "neo-Anabaptist" ethics of nonviolence that makes the church central. Their approach is better called an "ecclesial approach" because Jesus inaugurates a new

16. Karl Barth, *The Epistle to the Romans*, trans. Edwyn C. Hoskyns (London: Oxford University Press, 1968), 449.

17. *Apokalypse der deutschen Seele: Studien zu einer Lehre letzten Haltungen*, 3 vols. (Salzburg and Leipzig: Verlag Anton Pustet, 1937–1939).

era to which the church must bear witness. It primarily does so by refusing to use violence to control history. Rather than emphasizing a return to the specific land of Israel, they look to the condition of exile or diaspora as the way God wills the restoration of all things. The task of Israel and the church is to accept its condition of exile and follow the prophet Jeremiah's counsel in Jeremiah 29:4–7 (ESV):

> Thus says the Lord of hosts, the God of Israel, to all the exiles whom I have sent into exile from Jerusalem to Babylon: Build houses and live in them; plant gardens and eat their produce. Take wives and have sons and daughters; take wives for your sons, and give your daughters in marriage, that they may bear sons and daughters; multiply there, and do not decrease. But seek the welfare of the city where I have sent you into exile, and pray to the Lord on its behalf, for in its welfare you will find your welfare.

In 1954, the Mennonite theologian Yoder wrote an essay, "Peace without Eschatology," arguing that Jesus's eschatology makes sense of how we should live and act in the world. Yoder's eschatology draws heavily on Colossians 2:15 where Paul tells us that Jesus disarmed the "powers and principalities" or "rulers and authorities" and made a "spectacle" of them. In so doing, he "disarmed" them. The rulers and authorities are now part of an old age. The former age in which they claimed to be gods has been disarmed; they no longer have that kind of power over us. In crucifying Jesus, who was true God and humanity in one person, they were revealed for what they really are: self-absorbed centers of power who reject the things of God. Jesus calls and equips his church to be a sign of the new age, an age in which God's reign has begun and will be fulfilled in the eschaton. Meanwhile, Christians live in the midst of two eons: the new age of the church and the old age of the world. The rulers and authorities of the old age remain. They are creatures that serve God's purposes, but they have been limited in their role.

Yoder gives the following interpretation to the role for the rulers and authorities after Christ's triumph: "The Reign of Christ means for the state the obligation to serve God by encouraging the good and restraining evil, i.e. to serve peace, to preserve the social cohesion in which the leaven of the Gospel can build the church and also render the old aeon more tolerable."[18] The purpose of the ruling authorities has been limited by Christ's victory in his crucifixion, resurrection, and ascension. The real politics now resides with the church and all who witness to the new age that has been inaugurated and whose completion we await. Yoder states,

> The point apocalyptic makes is not only that people who wear crowns and who claim to foster justice by the sword are not as strong as they think – true as that is . . . It is that people who bear crosses are working with the grain of the universe. One does not come to that belief by reducing social processes to mechanical and statistical models, nor by winning some of one's battles for the control of one's own corner of the fallen world. One comes to it by sharing the life of those who sing about the Resurrection of the slain Lamb.[19]

The first task of Christians is to act within the new age that Christ has established. They act within it consistent with how Christ acted. It is the slain Lamb that can read from the scroll that discloses the "grain of the universe."

Eschatological Ethics: An Augustinian Approach

Few Christian ethicists link eschatology and ethics as do Yoder, Hauerwas, and McClendon. Few look to the book of Revelation for a political ethic, but the Anglican theologian Oliver O'Donovan is an exception. He too links eschatology, ecclesiology, ethics, and politics. In his *War and the American Difference*, Hauerwas acknowledges the similarities among O'Donovan, himself, and Yoder. He writes, "my (and John Howard Yoder's) understanding of the 'doctrine of the Two' shares more in common with O'Donovan than many might suspect."[20] By "the Two,"

---

18. John H. Yoder, *Christian Witness to the State*, Institute of Mennonite Studies Series, No. 3 (Newton, KS: Faith and Life Press, 1964), 5.

19. John H. Yoder, "Armaments and Eschatology," *Studies in Christian Ethics* 1/1 (Edinburgh: T&T Clark, 1988), 58. See also David Toole, *Waiting for God in Sarajevo* (Boulder, CO: Westview Press, 1998), 216; and Stanley Hauerwas, *With the Grain of the Universe* (Grand Rapids: Brazos, 2001), title page, 230–241.

20. Stanley Hauerwas, *War and the American Difference: Theological Reflections on Violence and National Identity* (Grand Rapids: Baker Academic, 2011), xii.

he means the doctrine of the two ages. While the ecclesial approach references this doctrine to argue that Christians should eschew violence, O'Donovan references it in order to advocate for just-war theory.

Rather than focusing on exile, however, O'Donovan focuses on the monarchy. It provides a political pattern that demonstrates what it means for Jesus to be "the desire of the nations." Every nation, explicitly or implicitly, now comes under his judgment. O'Donovan develops the work of one of the most important eschatological theologians in the Western tradition, St Augustine, and his doctrine of the two cities. Until the eschaton, the two cities – the city of God and the earthly city – exist side by side, the latter learning how to serve the former. It must still use violence, but for limited, political ends. These two approaches to ethics – the ecclesial and Augustinian – are perhaps the two theological approaches to the Christian life most indebted to the twentieth century's retrieval of eschatology for positive purposes.

For O'Donovan, the political significance of the book of Revelation is that the "authority of truth and justice" is now established, an authority that "political society on earth has consistently failed to achieve." This brings "God's word of judgment pronounced in Christ" as the "foundation for a new order of society."[21] The doctrine of the Two, he states, is, "before all else, a doctrine of two ages."[22] O'Donovan also links eschatology and ecclesiology. He writes, "John's eschatological approach to ecclesiology has this point in view: the root of any true political order, in which human beings can relate to God and to each other lovingly, is the conspicuous judgment of God. The good order of society is founded upon a judgment (*dikaiōma*), a declarative act which establishes a justice (*dikaiosune*). Without God's judgments we cannot comprehend how we may live together."[23] The church, then, is the "root" of true political community. But O'Donovan emphasizes the positive role of judgment by the rulers and authorities in the times between the times. In Christ's resurrection and ascension, creation is vindicated as good in and of itself. O'Donovan distinguishes creation from providence. Creation was always complete, good in and of itself. It has an order that does not need to develop or change. Providence is

21. Oliver O'Donovan and Joan Lockwood, *Bonds of Imperfection: Christian Politics Past and Present* (Grand Rapids: Eerdmans, 2004), 44.

22. Oliver O'Donovan, *The Desire of the Nations* (Cambridge: Cambridge University Press, 1996), 211.

23. O'Donovan and Lockwood, *Bonds of Imperfection*, 43.

the historical ordering by which God heals the wounds humans inflict in history.[24] Eschatology is the purpose toward which providence moves; it is "the vindication and perfection of the created order which was always there but never fully expressed."[25] Because John's Apocalypse unveils this purpose, it vindicates creation and reauthorizes secular authority. The rulers and authorities have been made subject to God's sovereignty in Christ, even if they do not know it; secular authority is reauthorized within its newly established limited role, learning in history to become subject. In the time between Christ's first and second comings, the secular authority exercises judgment, and, if necessary, it does so through force, coercion, and violence, but only for limited political ends. The eschatological conditions that reauthorize the secular at the same time limit state-sponsored violence.

Every thinker noted in the above section draws on the book of Revelation, the Apocalypse, to spell out an eschatological and ecclesiological ethic. Rather than teaching us to flee the world as some Western philosophers and theologians feared, it teaches us to engage it. Following Schweitzer, these thinkers interpret Jesus as an apocalyptic thinker. Contra Schweitzer, they do not find him to be a failed apocalyptic prophet. Through his resurrection and ascension, creation has been restored, although it still awaits its consummation. None of them focus on the land of Israel as necessary for that restoration in the time between the times. None of them distinguish eschatology from apocalypse. Several modern theologians, however, found it important to distinguish them in order to salvage eschatology from apocalyptic.

Eschatology without Apocalypse?

The German theologian Karl Rahner (1904–1984) was a Catholic contemporary to Balthasar. For him, eschatology is a necessary Christian doctrine that deals in general with last things and requires a "special hermeneutic" to interpret them, but apocalyptic claims to know too

---

24. See Oliver O'Donovan's earlier work, *Resurrection and Moral Order: An Outline for Evangelical Ethics* (Grand Rapids: Eerdmans, 1986), for his account of the vindication of creation and its relation to eschatology and history, especially 31–76.

25. O'Donovan, *Resurrection and Moral Order*, 53.

much about the end, and should be discarded.[26] Apocalyptic goes awry, he avers, because it is often interpreted as an "anticipatory, eyewitness account of a future which is still outstanding." This false hermeneutic leads to "avoidable" difficulties.[27] They are avoidable with a better interpretation. A proper hermeneutic begins not with prognostications about the future, but in "anticipation of what [the Christian] knows here and now about himself and about his salvific present." Or, put otherwise, Rahner states, "eschatology is man's view from the perspective of his experience of salvation, the experience which he now has in grace and in Christ."[28] Rahner worried about developing too much significance from apocalyptic.

The American Protestant theologian Charles Mathewes makes a similar distinction between eschatology and apocalyptic; he does so in part to question theologians like Hauerwas and Yoder for their apocalypticism. He sees detrimental consequences from apocalyptic thinking not only among theologians but also in much of the modern era, especially in American politics, anti-American jeremiads, and Marxist critiques. All, he argues, fall prey to the temptation to "apocalypticism." He distinguishes the "apocalyptic imagination" from "eschatological faith."[29] Like Rahner, Mathewes believes that apocalyptic goes bad when its defenders claim to know "in detail how things will turn out." This claim to know how things will turn out inhibits careful attention to the world as it is so that we might act in it with the confidence that "all will be well" without knowing how.[30]

Mathewes makes an important distinction between the way the world is and the way the world should be. An apocalyptic imagination assumes that it knows how the world should be, and thus it ignores

---

26. Karl Rahner, "The Hermeneutics of Eschatological Assertions," in *Theological Investigations*, vol. 4 (New York: Crossroad, 1982), 323–346. For a thorough investigation of the relation between apocalyptic and eschatology and their role in political theology, see Kyle Gingerich Hiebert, *The Architectonics of Hope: Violence, Apocalyptic and the Transformation of Political Theology* (Eugene: Cascade, 2017). He addresses Rahner's distinction and Metz's opposition to it on 30–44.

27. Karl Rahner, *Foundations of Christian Faith: An Introduction to the Idea of Christianity*, trans. William V. Dych (New York: Crossroad, 1987), 431.

28. Rahner, *Foundations of Christian Faith*, 432–433.

29. Charles T. Mathewes, *The Republic of Grace* (Grand Rapids: Eerdmans, 2010), 220–225.

30. Mathewes, *Republic of Grace*, 221. He makes similar claims in *A Theology of Public Life* (Cambridge: Cambridge University Press, 2007): see 18, 24, 38–39, 127.

acting in the world as it is. Because it acts in concert with an apocalyptic vision, it neglects careful attention to the way the world is and how we must act within it. The philosopher Jeffrey Stout agrees with Mathewes that living by an apocalyptic imagination can be dangerous to seeing and acting in the world as it is. "Some churches," he writes, "are so enraptured by utopian visions of the lion lying down with the lamb that they are unwittingly assisting actual lions in the destruction of actual lambs."[31] By distinguishing eschatology from apocalyptic Mathewes attempts to hold on to the importance of Christ's victory – all will be well – without it providing too much concrete guidance in addressing how the world is.

Assessing Apocalyptic Imaginings

Apocalyptic can go horribly awry, so the distinction between eschatology and apocalyptic is important. It goes awry when apocalyptic is interpreted as catastrophic. Rather than being transfigured into God's reign, material, historical reality must be destroyed in a conflagration for the sake of the new. Apocalyptic as *catastrophic* is both ancient and modern, often resulting from a millenarianism in which a thousand-year reign culminates in the coming of the antichrist (the latter term is not found in the Apocalypse). A diabolical ending to history produces a great tribulation.

Catastrophic apocalyptic thinking is not the best interpretation of apocalyptic. It too has led to significant errors. It was a source for serious political violence and inhuman activity in the sixteenth century, both by the Radical Reformers and against them. Christ's immanent return meant that everything we have – property, politics, relations, friendships, morals – should be held to lightly if at all, for it is coming to an end. But catastrophic apocalyptic was not unique to the sixteenth century; it continues into the modern era. It pervades the modern insofar as it assumes that the "modern," the new and improved, is about to arrive, and nothing we have done up to now has prepared us for its coming; it must all be discarded. Everything must be revised, discarded, rethought, reconstructed, possibly destroyed, for the old is always ob-

---

31. Jeffrey Stout, *Blessed Are the Organized: Grassroots Democracy in America* (Princeton: Princeton University Press, 2010), 42.

solete because of the new that is on the way. This apocalyptic tone is found in modern capitalism's "creative destruction" as well as in some historical performances of Marxism. The catastrophic apocalyptic represents an in-breaking that has no continuity with what came before. It positions the apocalypse in opposition to creation: creation provides no adequate knowledge for ethics or politics because the apocalyptic interruption does not perfect or complete creation; it destroys it.

The above discussion matters because apocalyptic thinking is not one thing. If it is understood as catastrophic, then Rahner's and Mathewes's distinction between eschatology and apocalyptic serves a useful purpose. If, rather than a catastrophe, apocalyptic is taken to be an *unveiling*, no such distinction is necessary. Instead, the important question is what kind of unveiling this is. Is it an unveiling that arises out of a fullness, affirming creaturely goods? Or is it an unveiling that negates, falling back unintentionally into the catastrophic?

Apocalypse from the Fullness of Worship

Apocalyptic arises from the fullness of a worshipful vision that uses images and symbols to show us a reality that could not otherwise be shown because it is something most of us do not see, and even if we do, we too easily lose sight of it. It shows us that the world as it appears to be is not what it is intended to be, and the world as it is intended to be is arriving in unexpected ways. The apocalyptic imagination does not counsel escapism, indifference, or withdrawal; it gives permission to act consistent with a vision partially unveiled.[32] The unveiling offers new possibilities for acting with the grain of the universe. As Michael Gorman says, the apocalyptic visionary "has seen what others have not; indeed he has seen Truth – invisible and future Truth – about the cosmos as it really is and really will be."[33] He has seen this in worship. Apocalyptic is worship and liturgy generating a theopolitical vision

---

32. Johann Metz wrote, "Imminent expectation will not let discipleship be postponed. It is not the apocalyptic feeling for life that makes us apathetic, but the evolutionistic!" Johann Metz, *Faith in History and Society: Toward a Practical Fundamental Theology*, trans. J. Matthew Ashley (New York: Herder & Herder, 2007), 163; cited in Gingerich Hiebert, *Architectonics of Hope*, 42.

33. Michael J. Gorman, *Reading Revelation Responsibly: Uncivil Worship and Witness – Following the Lamb into the New Creation* (Eugene: Cascade, 2011), 21–22.

that entails acting in harmony with that vision as best one can in the world as it is.

The apocalyptic imagination should frighten and alarm anyone and everyone who takes it upon her- or himself to hold power over others in order to rule and dominate them. For according to the Apocalypse, this class of people, politicians and merchants, the people we normally extol and thank for their service, can be seen in a very different light: as a beast with ten heads and seven horns. They risk standing on the side of the old age against the new age coming into existence, defending the world as it is rather than the world as it should be. The apocalyptic imagination performs what Richard Hays calls the "shock of reversal," because it is the slaughtered Lamb and not the "ferocious lion" who holds the key to unlock the truth of political order.[34] The war of the Lamb is not military conquest. It is a battle continuous with the politics present in the Sermon on the Mount. Its power and persuasive force are present in the means the Lamb uses, symbolized by the double-edged sword present in his mouth: his death and his "spoken word."[35] It should come as no surprise to careful readers of the Apocalypse that it gives us this word of caution: "if you kill with the sword, with the sword you must be killed" (Rev 13:10). Gorman succinctly states the theopolitical vision present in the apocalyptic imagination: "Revelation calls believers to nonretaliation and nonviolence, and not to a literal war of any sort, present or future. By its very nature as resistance, faithful nonconformity is not absolute withdrawal but rather critical engagement on very different terms from those of the status quo."[36] That is what the apocalyptic imagination asks of us.

The apocalyptic imagination can be well understood, as Beasley-Murray has put it, as political cartoon, depicting those convinced that they should take authority to control the levers of violent power as buffoons who are serving principalities and powers that they are unable to recognize.[37] The apocalyptic imagination is poetic, hyperbolic, comedic – and necessary, if our lives are not to be completely defined by the sword. The greatest comedic act of all is to love our enemies in their

34. See Richard Hays's *The Moral Vision of the New Testament: A Contemporary Introduction to New Testament Ethics* (San Francisco: HarperSanFrancisco, 1996), 174; and Gorman, *Reading Revelation Responsibly*, 108.

35. Gorman, *Reading Revelation Responsibly*, 109.

36. Gorman, 79.

37. Gorman, 19.

deadly seriousness, not take them too seriously, and let them know that there are alternative ways of being political than by dominating others.

And yet the apocalyptic imagination cannot primarily be a form of kenosis or resistance. The resistance must emerge as a secondary effect of its primary intention: to be infused with the overabundance of God's presence. It is out of this fullness that a proper humility and a lack of resentment gets generated, for resentment is always a sign that confidence is a sham. It is a sign of insecurity in which what one opposes is more determinative for who one is than what one is for. To be for something, to work from a fullness, does not require one opposing those on the "outside," for it is not weakness that directs us to them, but a fullness that dares to risk new forms of political engagement, forms that will find analogies that will be recognizable even in their difference. It works with the grain of the universe. The apocalyptic imagination is only for someone taken up into the ecstasy of worship.[38] "Worthy is the Lamb who was slain to receive power and wealth and wisdom and honor and glory and praise" (Rev 5:12 NIV).

Conclusion

Eschatology is the cultivation of an apocalyptic imagination through the fullness of vision present in worship. That vision is an *apocalypsis* – an unveiling that brings together the restoration of Israel, the coming of the kingdom or reign of God, and the renewal of creation. Much like the temple imagery present in Genesis 1, the unveiling reveals God's dwelling place and the creaturely dwelling place coming together in unity.

> See, the home of God is among mortals.
> He will dwell with them;
> they will be his peoples,
> and God himself will be with them;
> he will wipe every tear from their eyes.
> Death will be no more;
> mourning and crying and pain will be no more,
> for the first things have passed away. (Rev 21:3–4)

38. I owe this insight to Michael Gorman who writes that Revelation's "character as resistance literature is actually secondary to, and derivative of, its more fundamental character as worship literature, as a liturgical text" (Gorman, 25).

This unity cannot occur without final judgment, but the judgment is not for condemnation. It is so that every nation can bring its wealth and contribute to the unity God intends.

> I saw no temple in the city, for its temple is the Lord God the Almighty and the Lamb. And the city has no need of sun or moon to shine on it, for the glory of God is its light, and its lamp is the Lamb. The nations will walk by its light, and the kings of the earth will bring their glory into it. Its gates will never be shut by day – and there will be no night there. People will bring into it the glory and the honor of the nations. But nothing unclean will enter it, nor anyone who practices abomination or falsehood, but only those who are written in the Lamb's book of life. (Rev 21:22–27)

To act from this apocalyptic vision is to will the completion, fulfillment, or perfection of history.

For Further Reading

Barth, Karl. *The Epistle to the Romans.* Translated by Edwyn C. Hoskyns. London: Oxford University Press, 1968.

Gingerich Hiebert, Kyle. *The Architectonics of Hope: Violence, Apocalyptic and the Transformation of Political Theology.* Eugene: Cascade, 2017.

Gorman, Michael. *Reading Revelation Responsibly: Uncivil Worship and Witness – Following the Lamb into the New Creation.* Eugene: Cascade, 2011.

Hauerwas, Stanley. *Approaching the End: Eschatological Reflections on Church, Politics, and Life.* Grand Rapids: Eerdmans, 2013.

O'Regan, Cyril. *Theology and the Spaces of Apocalyptic.* Milwaukee: Marquette University Press, 2009.

Rahner, Karl. "The Hermeneutics of Eschatological Assertions." In *Theological Investigations*, vol. 4, 323–346. New York: Crossroad, 1982.

Toole, David. *Waiting for God in Sarajevo: Theological Reflections on Nihilism, Tragedy, and Apocalypse.* Boulder: Westview Press, 1998.

CHAPTER 2

The Past, the Present, and the Future of African Christianity: An Eschatological Vision for African Christianity

JAMES HENRY OWINO KOMBO

ABSTRACT

Eschatology in the African context remains a major driver of African Christian thought. Conversation around eschatology in Africa embraces the question of death and how the dead exist thereafter, and what the Christian faith says to these questions. The Hebrews 11 language of a "great cloud of witnesses" and the Nicene Creed's statement that "we look for the resurrection of the dead, and the life of the world to come," among other concepts, help anchor eschatology in the African context. Critical aspects of the African worldview – particularly (1) its approach to death, dying, and living on; (2) the question of the ancestors, spirits, and divinities; and (3) the modes of time, events, and seasons in African cosmology – are not just studies in sociology or anthropology, but collectively and individually are windows through which the idea of Christian eschatology may be brought to the African theological situation.

Eschatology: The African Worldview as a Theological Hermeneutic

This essay attempts to use a non-Western ontology, in this case an African worldview, to do theology for African Christianity. What is eschatology? How do I explain the term to my eighty-year-old father who, though not a theologian, does not use English, is not a *tabula rasa*, and has lived by the gospel for the better part of his life? "Eschatology" is a word foreign to African theological culture, though the concept it embodies is a religious principle that the African intellectual culture admits.[1]

The principles we take advantage of in articulating eschatology for African Christianity reside in the African worldview. In the African cultural traditions, we find permanent eschatological fixtures in death, dying, and living on; ancestors, spirits, and divinities; and time, events, and seasons. The way these categories stand in the African worldview allows us to do three things: (1) to see how pre-Christian Africa responded to these categories; (2) to view these notions and experiences as worthy ideas that are capable of being submitted to theological reflection in any forum; and (3) to bring unique African questions and responses to the global theological conversation.

This is all the more relevant given that eschatology is about physical death and its logical spin-off: What happens to people when they die? Not only does the question of time, events, and seasons in the context of this kind of eschatology allow for the utilization of the African ontology as a prism in relation to time, phenomena, and events, but these categories also help us to see how African Christianity is living out these aspects of the African world – what is time, for instance, in relation to death, ancestors, and the problem of relations? How is time related to the fulfillment of history realized in the corporate outlook of eschatology?

As J. S. Mbiti has argued, the shape of the African worldview is highly anthropocentric: "The human being is placed at the center of the cosmos, but not in an individualistic way. The individual is to be understood in terms of the kinship system to which he belongs. Our relationship thus comes before our individuality. The human being is thus seen not primarily as an autonomous individual, but as a person belonging to a group. He has specific, ongoing and permanent responsibilities towards the members of that group."[2] Mbiti outlines the African world as follows:

---

1. J. Page, *The Black Bishop* (London: Simpkin, 1910), 282.
2. Cited in William P. Russell, "'Time Also Moves Backwards': John Mbiti's Traditional Concept of Time and the Future of World Christianity," *Studies in World Christianity* 9 (2003): 88–102, here 96.

1. God, as the ultimate explanation of the genesis and sustenance of both humanity and all things;

2. Spirits, made up of superhuman beings and the spirits of human beings who died a long time ago;

3. Humans, both those who are alive and those about to be born;

4. Animals and plants, or the remainder of biological life;

5. Phenomena and objects without biological life.[3]

God occupies the number one category, since he is the Originator and Sustainer of humanity. The spirits, ancestors, and divinities explain the destiny of humanity: humans, who are ontologically below them, are ever moving inevitably toward them. Humanity's position at the very center of this ontology communicates human responsibility and relationships. The next two categories are animals and plants, and natural phenomena and objects. These categories provide both the means by and the theater in which human beings live. This ontology is experienced as a unified, integrated whole, incapable of being disturbed without destroying the entire ontology including the Creator.

In a world that is configured in these terms, how do we discern a solid eschatology for the Christian community therein? As we have noted, this ontology has a way of speaking to the categories named, and more specifically to the questions of personal eschatology, ancestors, and time. Although the African cultural traditions appear to have spoken so eloquently to these matters, rather than being theological the conversations have unfortunately remained at the ethnographic, linguistic, and historical levels. And so how we understand death, time, or ancestors – categories that themselves are richly theological – has contributed very little to the nature and shape of theological discourse, and much less to a probable approach for Christian eschatology for the African context. This must change, and theology, it appears, must start to take positive advantage of the constructs of the African intellectual culture.

---

3. J. S. Mbiti, *African Religions and Philosophy* (London: Heinemann, 1969), 20.

James Henry Owino Kombo

Eschatology in Relation to Death, Dying, and Living On

Africa is often caricatured as a space of death. The recent history of HIV and AIDS, long-term armed conflicts, civil wars, and genocide has led to so many deaths that thinking in these terms has only given this notion more currency. Consequently, as "in Europe after the First World War, mourning is replaced by memorialization, by the creation of museums and national memorial parks."[4] Another significant player in all this is the phenomenon of international migration which has necessitated new technologies such as refrigeration, embalmment, and use of media, particularly video and newspapers: it is reported that the insurance industry is making huge returns on account of these emerging practices. And so, although the "African way of death" is supposedly going the same way as the "American way of death," there are fundamental underlying differences.[5]

Evans-Pritchard thinks that the African funeral rituals are a reality in the African context because death in these societies provoked fear and revulsion. In the thinking of Evans-Pritchard, the dead could only find their place as ancestors, rather than vengeful ghosts, if their loss had been properly registered by their living relatives and the social groups around them. For Evans-Pritchard, therefore, the ultimate purpose of funeral customs was to allow the living relatives and social groups to get on with living.[6]

John S. Mbiti's understanding of the mourning process in Africa focuses on the need to connect the living to the living-dead ancestors and the spirits in the *sasa* and the *zamani*.[7] For him, in death we see "a separation and not annihilation; the dead person is suddenly cut off

---

4. Rebekah Lee, "Death and Dying in the History of Africa since 1800," *Journal of African History* 49 (2008): 342–343.

5. See Jessica Mitford's criticism of the American funeral industry, *The American Way of Death* (London: Simon & Schuster, 1963, rev. ed. 1998); cited in Gary Lederman, *Rest in Peace: Death and the Funeral Haven in Twentieth Century America* (Oxford: Oxford University Press, 2003).

6. Edward E. Evans-Pritchard, "Burial and Mortuary Rites of the Nuer," *African Affairs* 48 (1949): 51–63, here 62. See also on the misrepresentations of African beliefs about death, Louis-Vincent Thomas, *La mort africaine: Idéologie funéraire en Afrique noire* (Paris: Payot, 1982).

7. What is present is what is called *sasa*: this is the word for the time that covers the "now" period, with a sense of immediacy, newness, and nearness. The *zamani*, on the other hand, is the period of termination, the dimension in which everything finds

from the human society and yet the corporate group clings to him. This is shown through the elaborate funeral rites, the dirges and other ways of keeping in touch with the departed."[8] The dirge used by all African communities is a useful means of expressing the inevitable: the dead are praised, honored, and mourned.[9] In this case, therefore, the goal of life is the ability to begin a relationship with the world around – a sort of guaranteed open line for vibrant communication with both the visible and the invisible world. Thus the dead are granted a befitting funeral in which they are prevailed upon not to become wandering ghosts who suffer the indignity of not living properly after death.

We see here, therefore, a situation that takes the preeminence of death and its theology seriously. In the African approach to death and life beyond the grave, the culture has not only affirmed the reality of death, but it has also ensured that it has left no room for escaping or denying death and life thereafter.[10] The grounding in the African cosmology provides a framework through which we are able to face mortality for what it really is.

The manner in which African cosmology speaks to death and life beyond the grave makes it well suited to offer a new perspective to the wider church on death and life thereafter. Note that for the African situation, in death, the whole person and not just some part of the person continues to live and gets invested with powers to transact as an ancestor. And neither is death merely a private affair that one must face alone; instead, in death one becomes part of the "cloud of witnesses"

---

its halting point. See John S. Mbiti, *New Testament Eschatology in an African Background* (London: Oxford University Press, 1971), 23.

8. Mbiti, *African Religions and Philosophy*, 46.

9. African Christianity has traditionally not been happy with this – it has castigated elaborate funeral rituals, honoring the dead, and any form of maintenance of links with the dead either in the past or in the present. This continues to be a gray area, and Christians of independent, charismatic, and Pentecostal extraction appear to have sensed the lethargy of the historical forms of Christianity and are making steady inroads among the second-generation Christians.

10. I find the analysis of Rebekah Lee ("Death and Dying") cited here in full useful: "In the 1970s Philippe Aries argued that, whilst Europeans in the Middle Ages (like primitive peoples) accepted death as part of life, by the twentieth century they were more likely to attempt to deny it. A combination of industrialization, urbanization and the rise of scientific medicine eventually produced a situation in which death became a private affair, and one drained of meaning. Against this picture of death sanitized, medicalized and uneasily denied, African attitudes to death could be viewed with a degree of nostalgia" (342).

(see Heb 11). Thus, we continue with hope to learn that life exists beyond the grave. Christian theology talks of resurrected bodies which (1) have a physical nature and (2) are both immortal and imperishable (1 Cor 15:42–43). Elsewhere in Scripture, the immortal and imperishable body is also called a glorified and heavenly body (Phil 3:21; 1 John 3:2). What appears to have distinguished these realities from the pre-resurrection body is *not* immateriality, but the presence of both immortality and imperishability (1 Cor 15:42).

The doctrine of Christ's descent among the dead, though neglected among many traditions of the Christian faith, also offers a significant opportunity in this context. The central significance of this doctrine is its standing for us as a reminder of Christ's lordship over all and the liberation of the dead. By this doctrine, William P. Russell explains, Christ "liberates our relationships to our own dead, standing in the midst of them, removing all false fear and assuring us of the triumph of love. . . . Death thus has no victory and does not reduce our loving relationships to non-existence. Our relationships to our loved ones have not been terminated, but are now transformed in him."[11] This doctrine has tremendous pastoral potential for African Christianity given its traditional concern for dead relatives, and its recovery would also be an opportunity for African Christianity to spur a theological recovery of an equal significance to other parts of the world. Now we know that we do not have to fear our dead; on the contrary, Christ has liberated our relationship to the dead.

Ancestors, Spirits, and Divinities: Living in the Afterlife

The African world perceives interpenetration of the seen and the unseen, the visible and the invisible, the sacred and the secular.[12] Lamin Sanneh has focused the discussion on what he sees as Africa's religion, which falls like a shaft of light across the entire spectrum of life.[13] What this means for eschatology is that in the African world, we have ances-

---

11. Russell, "Time Also Moves Backwards," 96.

12. Stephen Ellis and Gerrie ter Haar, *Worlds of Power: Religious Thought and Political Practice in Africa* (New York: Oxford University Press, 2004), 14.

13. Lamin Sanneh, "New and Old in Africa's Religious Heritage: Islam, Christianity and the African Encounter," in *Exploring New Religious Movements: Essays in Honor of Harold Turner*, ed. Andrew F. Walls and Wilbert R. Shenk (Elkhart: Mission Focus, 1990), 64.

tors, spirits, and divinities living within the same space, environment, and plane. Moreover, we do not have another world which we are to occupy once we start talking of "the eschaton," and neither do we bracket eschatological matters in a far-distant future. Those who have already departed occupy abodes in proximity to their living relatives. The good men and women who die dream, at the very best, of becoming ancestors as soon as they transition so that they can continue to patronize their living relatives and acquaintances. It is thus understood that this is our world, and we continue to live in it whether we live or die.

Yet a fundamental question remains particularly problematic in African theology: Where do we go when we die? Where are our ancestors? This is a matter that generated tremendous heat and division between African evangelicals and other groups sometimes called "African ecumenists" in the mid-1970s to the 1980s. The evangelicals believed that J. S. Mbiti's three books – *African Philosophy and Religion* (1969), *The Concepts of God in Africa* (1970), and *New Testament Eschatology in an African Background: A Study of the Encounter between New Testament Theology and African Traditional Concepts* (1973) – were all built on the platform of theological universalism. Driven by this belief, there arose two responses spearheaded by Byang H. Kato's *Theological Pitfalls in Africa* (1975) and Tokunboh Adeyemo's *Salvation in African Tradition* (1979). Later, J. S. Mbiti would write *The Bible and Theology in African Christianity* (1987) in which he did two things: first, he laid out publicly his theology of Scripture; and, second, he specifically invited his theological interlocutors to a candid conversation. Thirty years later this conversation has still not happened, and the question of where our ancestors are remains unanswered.

In the interim, research appears to be unveiling several things: the ancestors and the spirits are not the nuisances they are sometimes thought to be. They raise an important theological question from a pre-Christian African point of view: What happens after we die? The import of this question must be seen from the position of someone who cares deeply about relations; a person who understands that relationships with our deceased relatives and with the world as it is known to us can be expressed in a myriad of ways; one who appreciates the idea that we are indeed moving very quickly to our ancestors who themselves are real people, and that the only thing that holds us back from being ancestors is the bridge of death standing between us; someone who appreciates that we and our deceased relatives may be in the *sasa* zone today, but soon we will together be in the graveyard of *zamani*. Thus we are not talking about ghosts (*pepo mbaya* – bad spirits), and neither are we talking of a mere system of ideas.

At the outset, it bears noting that while Africa has often been labeled as animistic,[14] rife with ancestor worship or veneration and existing in diffused monotheism, the meaningful application of all of these terms to the primal African worldview is contested.[15] While we cannot resolve all of these matters here, it is important to note up-front that the African relationship with ancestors is best understood not in the context of worship, at least as the term is biblically understood, but in the context of respect and relationship.

The living who relate to the ancestors may choose to communicate those relationships in active expressions, appropriations, and even experiences of the supernatural. Note that these beings – ancestors and the spirits – were once human beings living in the very same villages and holding positions of influence and honor. They live within easy proximity of their descendants and remain a part of their human family, which they continue to actively influence in either direction depending on the inclination or quality of the relationship.[16] Indeed, ancestors are part of the explanation of the African world giving meaning to benefits, misfortunes and to strains of life in society. They do this not just for the sake of it, but because they have immense interest in the welfare of their living descendants. Indeed Uchendu, in his anthropological study among the Igbo, does not just see the influence, but he also brings in what he calls the "equalitarian principle." He explains, "the reverence which the Igbo accord the ancestors has its definition in the transfer-

---

14. The term "animism" was coined by the anthropologist E. B. Tylor (1832–1917). By it he meant a theory of religion according to which religion is a "belief in spiritual beings" which originated in the early idea of attributing life, soul, or spirit to inanimate objects, "defining the religious systems of the lower races, so as to place them correctly in the history of culture," Tylor observed in 1892. See E. B. Tylor, "The Limits of Savage Religion," *Journal of the Royal Anthropological Institute* 21 (1892): 283–301.

15. Bolaji Idowu uses this concept to discuss the relationship between the divinities and Supreme Being in Africa according to which divinities serve as "functionaries in the theocratic government of the universe." Accordingly, therefore, the various divinities are apportioned respective duties to undertake in accordance with the will of the Supreme Being. It is also the case that divinities are ministers with different but complementary assignments in the monarchial government of the Supreme Being. Essentially, then, they are administrative heads of various departments. E. Bolaji Idowu, *African Traditional Religion: A Definition* (London: SCM, 1973), 170.

16. J. I. Omoregbe, *Ethics, a Systematic and Historical Study* (Lagos: Joja Educational Research and Publishers Ltd., 1993), 174–177, on Epicurean ethics.

ence of the social status of the elder of a kinship group into the realm of the spiritual where in the abode of the ancestors the former head of a family continues to retain the status and the attendant honour and respect which he enjoyed in his former earthly existence."[17]

Then there is the matter of vigilance – the notion that the ancestors keep watch over their living relatives. They reward but they could also punish in equal measure. Thus they focus on the requirement for discipline on the part of the living relatives and provision of guidance in matters of family affairs, traditions, and morality, as well as assurance of health and fertility. Thus witches, sorcerers, and bad medicine have no powers over a person whose ancestors are alert. But the ancestors and the spirits are also known to punish members of their family in cases of error and moral vice. To that extent, they are not only considered the ubiquitous part of the clan which links both the world we live in and the spirit world,[18] but they are also understood to possess supernatural powers donated to them by the Supreme Being. Thus, they can independently influence such powerful natural phenomena as rainfall and good harvests, and even the attainment of prosperity. On the other hand, such misfortunes as drought, famine, and destructive calamities may also be attributed to ancestors and the spirits.

In the African perspective, then, the dead are in active contact with their living relatives and acquaintances. This contact is seen in the context of providence, guidance, punishment, and protection. In such an environment, it makes sense for African Christianity to conceive eschatology not as some far-distant phenomenon, but as an aspect of the doctrine of the providence of God in the here and now. It should assert that God – not the ancestors, nor the spirits, nor the divinities – is the reason for rainfall, a good harvest, and even the attainment of prosperity. At the same time, as Russell notes, it should make space for the affirmation that, in death, "our relationships to our loved ones have not been terminated, but are now transformed in [Christ]." As

---

17. Victor C. Uchendu, *The Igbo of Southeast Nigeria* (New York: Holt, Rinehart and Winston, 1965), 19. See also F. A. Arinze, *Sacrifice in Igbo Religion* (Ibadan: Ibadan University Press, 1970), 19–20.

18. K. Amponsah, *Topics on West African Traditional Religion*, vol. 1 (Accra: McGraw-Hill FEP, 1974), 85. See also J. Omosadu Awolalu and P. Adelumo Dopamu, *West African Traditional Religion* (Ibadan: Onibonje Press, 1979), 272–273.

Christians, then, "we must henceforth see all these relationships as existing in Christ."[19]

Although divinities are generally not directly related to the African eschatological vision, they are of massive influence among many African communities, particularly in West Africa. These entities are known variously as "gods," "demigods," "nature spirits," divinities, and the like.[20] It is understood that they exist in the hundreds. For instance, among the Yoruba, there are as many as 201, 401, 600, or 1700 divinities.[21] Mbiti notes that among the Edo, there are as many divinities as there are human needs, activities, and experiences.[22] Their eschatological significance lies in the fact that they are perceived to be intermediaries between human beings and the Supreme Being. As such, they function as windows through which sacrifices, prayers, and offerings are both understood and presented to the Supreme Being. Although Idowu notes that they do not necessarily distract from direct worship of God, where they are part of reality, their abode and function is considered a halfway house, a purgatory of sorts, which by design is not supposed to be a permanent resting place for the departed.[23]

Interpreting Time, Events, and Seasons: Modalities of Space and Time

Africa's notion of eschatology is inextricably intertwined with time, events, and seasons. Here "time," whether past, present, or future, is understood as concrete and substantive. It is thus defined as "a composition of events which have occurred, those that are taking place now and those which are immediately to occur."[24] Time, it is explained, "is universally present, [however] conceptions and experiences of time themselves

19. Russell, "Time Also Moves Backwards," 96.
20. John S. Mbiti, *Concepts of God in Africa* (London: SPCK, 1975), 117.
21. Francis O. C. Njoku, *Essays in African Philosophy, Thought and Theology* (Owerri: Claretian Institute of Philosophy & Clacom Communication, 2002), 127.
22. Mbiti, *African Religions and Philosophy*, 119.
23. E. Bolaji Idowu, *Oludumare: God in Yoruba Belief* (London: Longmans, 1962).
24. Mbiti, *New Testament Eschatology*, 17. Also key to this view of time is Dominique Zahan, *Religion, spiritualité et pensée africaines*, 2nd ed. (Paris: Payot, 1970).

are not universal but rather historically and culturally contingent. They are dependent on and change with their respective contexts."[25]

It is now widely accepted that the main difference between African and European ideas of time is a recent development in European culture, which has redefined the future and given it absolute dominance in comparison to the past and the present. Indeed, as Reichardt argues, the "important elements which were used to distinguish European from African cultures in temporal terms in their strong and emphatic sense only emerged during the late eighteenth century."[26] Professor Mbiti appears to have followed this trend very closely in assigning minimal if any significance to the future as a category of time. Reichardt goes on to note that

> time in traditional African societies is radically contextual. In a small subsistence economy and small village or tribal units, the mechanics and logistics of the coordination of people's actions and the community's functioning does not presuppose an abstract time scheme; the network of actions can still be coordinated by word of mouth and face-to-face interaction. Consequently, there is no idea of rational, abstract and mechanical time; rather, time is intimately linked with events, rituals, natural cycles, and the supernatural. Time is not understood as being under the control of human beings, not something to be shaped or filled; it is a dimension of the surrounding world, including the gods.[27]

This characterization that compounds time alongside God, events, activities, and seasons allows for a possibility of conceiving potential time and actual time. But more importantly, this conception of time, Mbiti argues, is "the key to our understanding of the basic religious

25. Ulfried Reichardt, "Time and the African-American Experience: The Problem of Chronocentrison," *American Studies* 45, no. 4 (2000): 465.

26. Reichardt, "Time," 469.

27. Reichardt, 470. Note also that modern philosophical considerations of time (Henri Bergson, William James, John Dewey, George Herbert Mead, and Alfred North Whitehead) and contemporary theories of time all offer critiques of mechanical time and point out the contextual character of time. This insight is seen in William Faulkner's novels. Mechanical time is no longer considered objective; as Niklas Luhmann points out, time is now used by systems as a medium of their operations. Thus, there is no objective time. What we have now is system-specific time.

and philosophical concepts."[28] There are seven philosophical notions involved here, namely, (1) that we are moving backwards in time toward the past and we are slowly but surely becoming part of it – time thus moves backwards rather than forward; (2) the past to which we are moving belongs to the ancestors and the spirits; (3) on account of this movement, the living dead are our immediate horizon – they are our future. This conception of time is (4) essentially relational. As such, we retain our relationships even in death; death does not redefine or delete how we relate. These relationships (5) nevertheless are not only multiple, but they are also accentuated in different ways. The time component, as previously noted, is divided into two: (6) *zamani* and *sasa*. In all this, (7) human beings are at the center because they have permanent responsibilities.

It is on this ground that Mbiti argues that time is measured by events.[29] Thus, time is not conceived in a vacuum; rather we say that it is "time for," "time to," or a "time of." Time in this case is designated and not merely numerical or mathematical. Thus, we do not become slaves of time – we master time. In this scheme of things, therefore, calendars represent phenomena – concrete things that happened. For instance, an "oldman" remembers when he was born or when he married in relation to an event or a phenomenon that happened at around the same time. Time becomes a significant marker of events or phenomena. In the case of our "oldman," what is important is that he was born or that he married, not the mathematical exactitude which characterizes the year or month. That time is meaningful only to the extent that he was born or married then; it is a mere beacon in the theater of events.

This conception of time has significant theological consequences. Russell raises questions that deserve further study: "is this view of time compatible with the Christian faith, or not? What insight into faith does it help us to grasp better? What error does it contain that the Christian faith corrects?"[30]

---

28. In Joseph K. Adjaye, "Time in Africa and Its Diaspora: An Introduction," *Time in the Black Experience*, ed. Joseph K. Adjaye (Westport: Greenwood Press, 1994), 5.

29. Mbiti, *African Religions and Philosophy*, 19–22.

30. Russell, "Time Also Moves Backwards," 89.

Contact Points

It is now well demonstrated that Christianity is a worldwide phenomenon. As such, it now operates within the contours of a new theological culture that embraces all Christian traditions while at the same time flourishing in the intellectual constructs of Africa, Asia, Latin America, and Oceania. This has been described as "worldwide theology."[31] According to this scheme of things, Christian thought from the cultural margins like Africa and Asia will increasingly manifest an active engagement with historical voices. Thus, African ideas about death, ancestors, spirits, time, and events "will influence theological thinking beyond Africa and may help to resolve ancient conflicts that have divided Christians in the past."[32] Speaking specifically to Mbiti's conception of time, Russell argues that its adequacy should be judged by "whether or not, and in what ways, it might help us to understand better the Christian revelation. The ethnographic, linguistic and historical questions that have dominated the discussion of the idea so far thus recede into the background."[33] In light of the matters discussed here, I now highlight six areas in which African Christian thought may have a salutary impact on wider Christian theology.

The Idea of Time

Generally, the idea of time is under-researched. In particular, its relationship to context and culture, particularly the African culture, has been generally ignored, leaving in focus only a relatively recent notion of time made popular in modernity. This was already recognized in the 1980s and the 1990s, and today nothing much has happened to change the state of affairs. Some of the outstanding contributions during this period include J. T. Fraser's authoritative publication *The Voices of Time* (1981) "included contributions on 'non-Western' societies like China and India but conspicuously omitted Africa."[34] Whereas there is a need to fill the gap and bring Africa into the picture, such studies should not merely be critiques of John Mbiti and Dominique Zahan and what they

31. Russell, 89.
32. Russell, 89.
33. Russell, 89.
34. Adjaye, "Time in Africa and Its Diaspora," 7–8.

saw of time in the late 1960s and the early 1970s. Instead, further study should focus on time as a multifaceted and contextual phenomenon that is intimately linked and significantly related to events, rituals, natural cycles, and the supernatural. The relational aspect of time is particularly critical: we stand in relation to our deceased relatives, who are our future since we are moving toward them; we stand in relation to God; and we stand in relation to the rest of God's creation.

Relationships

The issue here is the reality of the living, the ancestors, and the spirits in African ontology and the fact that the living and the dead in fact stand in a permanent and ongoing relationship. In this case, therefore, relationship as a phenomenon is to be viewed as an epistemic handle. The epistemic and eschatological challenge posed by relationship as entrenched in African ontology is itself a matter that African Christianity and worldwide theology will have to deal with. Is it ancestor worship – is it ancestor veneration?[35] What does Scripture say about the relationship between the living and the dead? What relationships are condemned and which ones may be permitted? Don't we encounter God as a God of ancestors? Isn't he a God of the living, not of the dead? In any case, Israel followed their ancestors in faith; we see a similar thing in the case of the Christians in the New Testament in the manner in which they related to the apostles, and in the church communities the apostles founded. These questions and many more in the context of relationships as a hermeneutical key may require a new attitude, even perhaps a totally new effort toward another way of looking at the relationship between the living and the dead.

Universalism

An observation was made above about the supposed rift among theology scholars in Africa on the basis of what was understood as universalism. The question was not a Christian theology question, but an Afri-

---

35. C. S. Bae, "Ancestor Worship and the Challenges It Poses to the Christian Mission and Ministry," PhD diss. (University of Pretoria, 2007), 1.

can ontology question: Where do we go when we die? Where are our ancestors? Mbiti posed these questions in his books *African Philosophy and Religion* (1969), *The Concepts of God in Africa* (1970), and *New Testament Eschatology in an African Background: A Study of the Encounter between New Testament Theology and African Traditional Concepts* (1973). He subsequently received swift responses from Byang H. Kato's *Theological Pitfalls in Africa* (1975) and Tokunboh Adeyemo's *Salvation in African Tradition* (1979). Later, as mentioned above, Mbiti attempted a truce through his book *The Bible and Theology in African Christianity* (1987), in which he laid out publicly his theory of Scripture and then proceeded to invite his theological interlocutors to a candid conversation. Thirty years later this conversation has still not happened, and the ontological question of where our ancestors are and in what way we might relate with them is largely unanswered.

It appears to me that there are two parallel questions here: eschatology and soteriology. Whereas Byang Kato and Adeyemo appear to be driving at an evangelical soteriological question, Mbiti is pursuing an eschatological agenda informed by his notion of time and relations.[36]

The Doctrine of Christ's Descent among the Dead

This doctrine, which is part of the church's creedal tradition, has often been abandoned in reflections on eschatology due to numerous historical and exegetical puzzles it presents. Fortunately, due to the historical link between African Christianity and its doctrine that the dead remain alive, the controversy associated with this doctrine is minimized and the significance of this doctrine for eschatology remains. African Christian faith seems very ready to work towards a strong doctrine of "Descent among the Dead." Note that what this doctrine does is to explain how Christ's time in the tomb helps locate his atoning work within the doctrine of the last things. The robust conversation about the ancestors and the spirits is, in my opinion, an opportunity to once again attend to the doctrine of Christ's descent among the dead. The doctrine remains

---

36. Note that the *Roho* Christian denomination spread all over East Africa hardly consider themselves saved, and yet they wear turbans and scarves bearing the conspicuous mark of the cross, and they call each other *japolo* (meaning "people of heaven"). The *Tukutendereza*, on the other hand, are a product of the Puritan movement and believe in the salvation wrought by Jesus Christ and confession of sins.

significant both for its pastoral potential and for its standing for us as a reminder of Christ's lordship over all, including the dead, and his liberation of the dead.

By adopting this orphaned doctrine and reinterpreting it in light of the African theological culture and raising it to the global church, African Christianity would be making a contribution which it alone is prepared to make at the moment – namely to declare that Christ "liberates our relationships to our own dead, standing in the midst of them, removing all false fear and assuring us of the triumph of love. . . . Death thus has no victory and does not reduce our loving relationships to nonexistence. Our relationships to our loved ones have not been terminated, but are now transformed in him."[37] We need to take up this challenge, and we need to demonstrate its relevance to African Christianity both for pastoral reasons and for the benefit of the global church.

Reassessing Sixteenth-Century Eschatological Controversies

The church in the sixteenth century provided answers to several eschatological questions, including those raised by the Catholic doctrine of acquisition of merit, the doctrine of indulgences, the idea of the communion of the saints, the idea of purgatory, as well as the Reformers' response to prayers to and for the dead. These well-considered answers addressed the situation of Europe and the questions raised at that time. They were specific to the issues at hand and are not in any way related to the African notions of death, dying, ancestors, spirits, time, events, and seasons studied here. It is therefore inappropriate to link these concepts articulated in the sixteenth century as answers to specific African questions.

The African eschatological ideas discussed here are independent and have their own unique origin and meaning. As Russell argues, the African concepts raised in the context of our own ontology "ought not to be understood in terms of a dispute that is foreign to it."[38] What the Catholics and the Reformers intended to achieve by their responses to eschatological controversies at the time was an appropriate understand-

---

37. Russell, "Time Also Moves Backwards," 96.
38. Russell, 91.

ing of Paul's doctrine of justification; the African agenda as demonstrated in this work is primarily cosmological and only secondarily pastoral.

Christ as an Ancestor

Ancestors play an important role in African cosmology. As far as these ontologies are concerned, ancestors are deceased members of a community who live within easy proximity of their living relatives and acquaintances as they provide guardianship and support. Many theologians have borrowed the term "ancestor" from respective cultures of reception and used it as a handle for Christ.

Eschatological and Trinitarian thinking informs us differently: Jesus is one with the Father and the Holy Spirit in the Godhead. He is God himself. He is not an elevated ancestor, nor is he a Great Ancestor.[39] In African cosmology, ancestors occupy a category below God but above human beings. Christ stands in the midst of ancestors, not as one of them but as "*other*," "removing all false fear and assuring us of the triumph of love."[40] Because of the work of this Christ, death even for the ancestors themselves is defeated, and our relationships with deceased relatives are not terminated nor reduced to nonexistence. On the contrary, "our relationships with our deceased loved ones are now transformed in him."[41]

Conclusion

Conversations around eschatology in African Christianity have unfortunately been shrunk to a play whose main plot is time and character. We applaud Mbiti for his illustrious and tireless contributions, spanning

---

39. Note the three distinct functions of ancestors: "liturgical companions to the living"; mediators between God and human beings; and guardians of family affairs, traditions, ethics, and activities. In view of these functions divergent views arise on whether or not Christ can be called an ancestor. John Pobee and Bujo readily state that Jesus could be called an ancestor (see Diane Stinton, *Jesus of Africa: Voices of Contemporary African Christologies* [Nairobi: Paulines Publications Africa, 2004], 140–143); Nürnberger disagrees (see K. Nürnberger, *The Living Dead and the Living God* [Pietermaritzburg: Cluster Publications, 2007], 234); while Stinton is noncommittal (see Stinton, *Jesus of Africa*, 165).

40. Russell, "Time Also Moves Backwards," 96.

41. Russell, 96.

many decades, to the development of African Christian thought. But African Christianity must now expand its field of play and consciously include more contributors to the conversation while, at the same time, expanding the agenda of eschatology beyond just time. Already, as we have seen, more in the African Christian culture could be and has been discussed: death, dying, and life beyond the grave; ancestors, spirits, and divinities; time, events, and seasons. These are not just issues of philosophy, religious studies, and social sciences – though they have at times been dragged and confined to these corners. These are conversations in eschatology, and where we have processed them as theological responses we must utilize them for pastoral concerns, and allow them to inform the thought of worldwide Christianity.

For Further Reading

Adjaye, Joseph K. "Time in Africa and Its Diaspora: An Introduction." *Time in the Black Experience.* Ed. Joseph K. Adjaye. Westport: Greenwood Press, 1994.

Bae, C. S. "Ancestor Worship and the Challenges It Poses to the Christian Mission and Ministry." PhD thesis, University of Pretoria, 2007.

Evans-Pritchard, Edward E. "Burial and Mortuary Rites of the Nuer." *African Affairs* 48 (1949): 51–63.

Lee, Rebekah. "Death and Dying in the History of Africa since 1800." *Journal of African History* 49 (2008): 342–359.

Mbiti, John S. *New Testament Eschatology in an African Background.* London: Oxford University Press, 1971.

Nürnberger, K. *The Living Dead and the Living God.* Pietermaritzburg: Cluster, 2007.

Reichardt, Ulfried, "Time and the African-American Experience: The Problem of Chronocentrism." *American Studies* 45, no. 4 (2000): 465–484.

Russell, William P. "'Time Also Moves Backwards': John Mbiti's Traditional Concept of Time and the Future of World Christianity." *Studies in World Christianity* 9 (2003): 88–102.

Tempels, Placide. *Bantu Philosophy.* Paris: Présence Africaine, 1969.

CHAPTER 3

Revelation 21:1–4 from an African Perspective

JOHN D. K. EKEM

ABSTRACT

Apocalyptic theology constitutes a key component of biblical eschatology. Unfortunately, it is a neglected area or at best "an endangered species" in African biblical scholarship. This chapter critically examines Revelation 21:1–4, one of the most popular texts that has attracted a variety of interpretations on the Ghanaian Christian terrain. This essay argues that eschatological issues emerging from the text have a strong bearing on current African sociopolitical, economic, and religious realities, including ecological conservation.

Introduction

The interpretation of apocalyptic literature tends to open Pandora's box for biblical scholarship. Texts emerging from this type of literature, as exemplified in Revelation, have attracted a variety of interpretations at academic and nonacademic levels, depending on whether one subscribes to the amillennial, premillennial, millennial, or postmillennial school of thought or to approaches that may be described as Preterist, Historicist, Futurist, or Idealist.[1] In the wake of eschatological speculations about how the world will come to an end and the proliferation of

---

1. For a discussion of different hermeneutical approaches to the text of Revelation, see Frederick D. Mazzaferri, *The Genre of the Book of Revelation from a Source-Critical Perspective* (Berlin: Walter de Gruyter, 1989), 33–34; David L. Barr, ed., *Reading the Book of Revelation* (Atlanta: Society of Biblical Literature, 2003), 1–6.

books and movies on the subject,[2] an investigation of the nature and significance of apocalyptic texts assumes special importance.

The study and application of such a literary genre to current realities in church and society has emerged as a delicate hermeneutical exercise. Unfortunately, some forms of reading methods or hermeneutical approaches to apocalyptic passages have generated unwarranted extremism such as religious fanaticism, or apathy in matters of social and political involvement. Unfamiliarity with critical tools for interpreting such literature has, thus, turned out to be counterproductive. A proper understanding, analysis, and repackaging of apocalyptic texts for specific audiences will positively impact global efforts at social justice and peaceful coexistence.

As a case study, this chapter examines Revelation 21:1–4 that has often served as a beacon of hope for those in distressing situations, particularly in Africa, where multiple challenges confront people in the social, religious, political, and economic spheres.

The proposed hermeneutical approach for this study can be described as eclectic insofar as methods of reading behind the text, within the text, and in front of the text are brought on board to highlight specific issues. To be precise, we can hardly do justice to the text under consideration without coming to grips with its historical, rhetorical, and current contextual nuances.

Locating Revelation within the Context of Apocalyptic Literature

The Judeo-Christian Scriptures contain a variety of literary genres that have engendered extensive scholarly discussions. We can, for example, make mention of Deuteronomic, prophetic, and wisdom literature, as well as Gospel, apologetic, and epistolary material. Each of these has its own characteristics, some of which overlap with others, and critical scholarly tools are needed to determine their *Sitz im Leben*.

Significantly, apocalyptic literature contains aspects of the above-mentioned literary genres whilst remaining distinct from them in certain respects. Within the apocalyptic literary genre itself, we can

---

2. See, for example, Hal Lindsey, *The Late Great Planet Earth* (Grand Rapids: Zondervan, 1970).

identify two main approaches: those that focus primarily on "reviews of history" (e.g., Daniel, Jubilees, 4 Ezra, and 2 Baruch) and those that highlight "otherworldly journeys" (e.g., the Testament of Abraham, Testament of Levi 2–5, and the Apocalypse of Zephaniah).[3] With the help of symbolic language and several literary devices, apocalyptic writers build their message around the following themes:

1. Dualism, whereby a sharp distinction is drawn between good and evil, light and darkness, heaven and earth, "this world" and "the world to come";

2. God's sovereignty over history and the cosmos;

3. Ultimate vindication of the righteous;

4. Access to divine revelation through intermediary heavenly beings;

5. Enduring optimism;

6. Opening of a new chapter in creation.

As a key text in the apocalyptic literary genre and the most popular material for some Christian interpretations of the "end times," Revelation appears to combine features of all of the above. Apocalyptic material thrives amidst persecution and other forms of traumatic experience on the part of its addressees. Thus, while scholars view the material in Daniel, especially chapters 7–12, against the backdrop of the Maccabean revolt, Revelation is often interpreted in the context of persecution and martyrdom of Christian communities in the first-century Greco-Roman world. Hendriksen, for instance, considers the purpose of Revelation to be an attempt to "comfort the militant Church in its struggle against the forces of evil."[4] Apocalyptic theologies as envisioned in Daniel and Revelation raise the question of "theodicy," the sovereignty of God vis-à-vis the persistence of evil. But their authors try to resolve this ambiguity by pointing to the transient nature of evil phenomena and the fact that God has the final word. Within the canon, Isaiah 24–27 and 56–66; Ezekiel; Joel 2:28 – 3:21; Zechariah 9–14; Mark 13 (and Matt 24; Luke 21:5–36); 1 Thessalonians 4:13 – 5:11; 2 Thessalonians 2:1–12;

---

3. For a concise but very useful discussion, see Carl R. Holladay, *Introduction to the New Testament* (Waco: Baylor University Press, 2017), 837–841.

4. William Hendriksen, *More Than Conquerors. An Interpretation of the Book of Revelation* (Grand Rapids: Baker, 2015), 13.

2 Peter 2–3; and Jude also contain interesting ingredients of apocalyptic material. Holladay sums it up:

> Revelation has long been recognized as an apocalyptic writing whose language and outlook resonate with these other biblical and non-biblical apocalyptic writings, which were produced between 200 BCE and 200 CE . . . As the vast body of Jewish and Christian apocalypses became available in critical editions and translations, scholars were able to gain a better understanding of how apocalyptic literature worked, what symbols and images it tended to use, how it related to biblical prophetic books, and what circumstances produced such writings. Understanding the "rules" of apocalyptic writing and how apocalyptic thinkers construed their world enabled scholars to interpret Revelation within the broader context of the ancient world.[5]

The rhetorical nuances of Revelation, with its use of symbolism to respond to a crisis situation in the first-century CE, call for a careful approach to the text.[6]

While recognizing some historical realities such as persecution and martyrdom of Christians during the reign of latter first-century CE Roman emperors, we should guard against biblicist-literalistic and allegorical interpretations that carry the danger of unhealthy speculations. Succumbing to the latter does obvious violence to the author's rhetoric of "Divine Sovereignty Trump Card" as antidote to the wider negative forces of darkness, dehumanization, wanton destruction of nature, corruptibility, and death. The text of Revelation can be outlined as follows:[7]

> Prologue and Opening Vision of Christ (1:1 – 3:22)
> Opening Heavenly Vision (4:1 – 5:14)
> The Lamb Opens the Seven Seals (6:1 – 8:5)
> The Seven Trumpets (8:6 – 11:19)
> Miscellaneous Visions (12:1 – 14:20)

5. Holladay, *Introduction to the New Testament*, 838.

6. For an interesting discussion, see Steven J. Friesen, *Imperial Cults and the Apocalypse of John: Reading Revelation in the Ruins* (Oxford: Oxford University Press, 2001); Young Jang, "Narrative Function of the Apocalypse," *Scriptura* 80 (2002): 186–196. Another useful reading is George Eldon Ladd, *The Presence of the Future: The Eschatology of Biblical Realism* (London: SPCK, 1981).

7. Extracted from Holladay, *Introduction to the New Testament*, 850–851.

Seven Angels, Seven Plagues, Seven Bowls of Wrath
(15:1 – 16:21)
The Fall of Babylon (17:1 – 19:10)
Final Visions and Epilogue (19:11 – 22:21)

The Text of Revelation 21:1–4: Some Concise Exegetical Remarks

Author's Translation

1. And I saw a new heaven and a new earth. For the former heaven and the former earth have gone out of existence and the sea was no more.

2. And I saw the holy city, [namely], the new Jerusalem, coming down out of heaven from God, prepared as a bride adorned for her husband.

3. And I heard a great voice from the throne saying, "Behold the tabernacle of God is with humankind, and he shall dwell [pitch his tent] with them, and they shall be his people, and God himself shall be with them [as their God],

4. And he shall wipe away every tear from their eyes, and death shall be no more; neither shall there be weeping nor crying nor pain any more, [because] the former things have passed away.

Concise Exegesis

Chapter 21 ushers us into a *Theologie der Hoffnung* (Theology of Hope), to borrow Jürgen Moltmann's famous title. Following a gloomy picture of judgment and the destruction of whatever constitutes opposition to God's sovereignty and salvific plan, including death and Hades (20:14), the apocalyptic writer escorts us to witness an interventionist holistic salvific act of God. This is described in vivid terms as the sight of a new heaven and a new earth (21:1a). In order to erase any doubts regarding the possible threat of anti-godly corruptible phenomena, attention is drawn to the previous heaven and the previous earth passing out of existence (21:1b). The sea that symbolizes a threat to the divine scheme of things is also no more (21:1c). But what exactly is the nature of this new heaven and new earth? This has been interpreted in various ways. One school of thought posits that the new heaven and the new earth will be newly created and, for that matter, radically different from the previous ones that have gone out of existence.[8] Walvoord describes it as an act of new creation rather than a renovation.[9] Another school of thought holds the view that the new heaven and the new earth will be a renewal or transformation of the previous ones that have been corrupted by sin.[10] According to Smith, the old heaven and earth will not vanish into nothingness.[11] Morris describes the process as the "complete transformation of all things,"[12] and Blount views this as a process of radical continuity characterized by a radically transformed earth.[13] A third school of thought interprets the phrase "a new heaven and a new earth" (21:1a) in a metaphorical sense as a reference to the moral and spiritual transformation of the world.[14] Without necessarily taking a specific stand, Fee cautions against a literal reading of the text.[15] The expression "and the sea was no more" (21:1c) has also been interpreted literally and metaphorically. The literal reading postulates that the new earth will not have a sea in it.[16] According to Walvoord, the only water

8. John Walvoord, *The Revelation of Jesus Christ* (Chicago: Moody, 1966), 311–313; Ben Witherington III, *Revelation*, New Cambridge Commentary (Cambridge: Cambridge University Press, 2003), 252–253; Margaret Barker, *The Revelation of Jesus Christ* (Edinburgh: T&T Clark, 2000).

9. Walvoord, *Revelation of Jesus Christ*, 311.

10. John Philips, *Exploring Revelation* (Chicago: Moody, 1974), 263–264; Michael Wilcock, *The Message of Revelation: I Saw Heaven Opened* (Nottingham: Inter-Varsity Press, 1975), 197–199; Robert Mulholland, *Holy Living in an Unholy World: Revelation* (Grand Rapids: Zondervan, 1990), 315; Graeme Goldsworthy, *The Gospel in Revelation: Gospel and Apocalypse* (Carlisle: Paternoster, 1994), 132–138; G. K. Beale, *Revelation: A Shorter Commentary* (Grand Rapids: Eerdmans, 2015), 497.

11. J. B. Smith, *A Revelation of Jesus Christ: A Commentary on the Book of Revelation* (Scottdale: Herald, 1961), 281.

12. Leon Morris, *Revelation: An Introduction and Commentary* (Leicester: Inter-Varsity Press, 1976), 243.

13. Brian K. Blount, *Revelation: A Commentary* (Louisville: John Knox Press, 2009), 376.

14. Charles R. Erdman, *The Revelation of John* (Philadelphia: Westminster Press, 1929), 154; J. M. Ford, *Revelation: Introduction, Translation and Commentary* (New York: Doubleday, 1975), 360–362.

15. Gordon Fee, *Revelation: A New Covenant Commentary* (Cambridge: Lutterworth, 2011), 290–293.

16. Philips, *Exploring Revelation*, 263–264; Walvoord, *Revelation of Jesus Christ*, 311.

body will be the river mentioned in Revelation 22:1.[17] Philips interprets it as a symbolic reference to the Holy Spirit.[18] One can also interpret it as a Johannine apocalyptic symbol of chaos and evil or anything that is contrary to God's salvific will and opposes God's sovereignty.[19] Wilcock alludes to the fact that in ancient mythologies, the sea was representative of the chaos monster Tiamat.[20] Similar to the *Odyssey* in Greek mythology, the sea personifies evil which must be abolished. Keener has also come up with the intriguing suggestion that the disappearance of the sea in John's apocalyptic vision is a probable reference to the end of all human mercantile trade, since God will supply all the needs of his people.[21] It should, therefore, come as no surprise to us that in the Johannine apocalyptic scheme of things, it disappears from the new order of creation.[22] It is quite obvious from these varied perspectives that there is no consensus regarding the interpretation of Revelation 21:1, even though an overly literal interpretation fails to capture the message the apocalyptic writer is trying to put across by means of symbolic language.

With reference to 21:2 which deals with the motif of the New Jerusalem, Philips, Smith, and Walvoord share the view that it is a celestial city inhabited by God's sanctified ones, and that this is in keeping with Christ's promise to prepare a place for all believers.[23] Walvoord opines that it hangs like a satellite that God has already prepared.[24] But there is also the literal messianic view that this New Jerusalem is a qualitative restoration of the earthly Jerusalem which was destroyed.[25] Another school of thought represented by Morris, Fee, Goldsworthy, and Mulholland interprets "the holy city" introduced in apposition to the "New Jerusalem" as a metaphorical reference to a radically renewed commu-

---

17. Walvoord, *Revelation of Jesus Christ*, 311.

18. Philips, *Exploring Revelation*, 272–273.

19. Wilcock, *Message of Revelation*, 198; Witherington III, *Revelation*, 253; Erdman, *Revelation of John*, 155; Ford, *Revelation*, 361; Morris, *Revelation*, 243; Blount, *Revelation*, 377.

20. Wilcock, *Message of Revelation*, 198.

21. Craig S. Keener, *Revelation*, NIV Application Commentary (Grand Rapids: Zondervan, 2000), 406.

22. Fee, *Revelation*, 292.

23. Philips, *Exploring Revelation*, 264; Smith, *Revelation of Jesus Christ*, 282; Walvoord, *Revelation of Jesus Christ*, 313.

24. Walvoord, *Revelation of Jesus Christ*, 313.

25. R. H. Charles, *A Critical and Exegetical Commentary on the Revelation of St John* (New York: Charles Scribner & Sons, 1920), 2: 200–201.

nity of human existence that becomes the climax of God's regenerative work among mortals, with the church serving as a paradigm.[26] Contrary to Walvoord's view that it is a prepared "hidden satellite," Blount states categorically that the New Jerusalem is "this-worldly" and not "otherworldly."[27] Its uniqueness lies in the fact that it is God who takes the initiative to renew his creation. Middleton poses the question as to whether the ushering in of a new cosmos presupposes "an obliteration followed by replacement or a reference to some form of (admittedly radical) transformation."[28] Basing his discussion on the use of the verb *parēlthen* ("has passed away") to qualify *ta archaia* ("the old things") in 2 Corinthians 5:17, he argues that this does not in any way connote obliteration. "By analogy, then, the passing away of the present heaven and earth to make way for the new creation is also transformative and not a matter of destruction followed by replacement."[29] Nevertheless, we cannot overlook the influence of apocalyptically loaded prophetic material from Isaiah and Ezekiel on the "theology of radical renewal" in Revelation. Mathewson has done a thorough study of passages from Isaiah 25:8; 60:1–22; 61:10; 65:15–20; and Ezekiel 40–48 that has a bearing on issues raised by the apocalyptic author of Revelation. Along with others, he observes: "By this density of Isaian texts utilized according to thematic patterns throughout Revelation, as well as the anticipatory use of Isaian oracles of renewal and the new Jerusalem, John has once again prepared the reader for and has created an expectation of a reuse of Isaian texts relating to eschatological salvation, renewal and the new Jerusalem in the final chapters of Revelation."[30]

In Mathewson's opinion, in Revelation 21 the author tries to draw a sharp contrast between two epochs: the present order that characterizes corruptibility, and the coming new order that is a qualitatively superior

---

26. Mulholland, *Holy Living in an Unholy World*, 316; Goldsworthy, *Gospel in Revelation*, 137; Morris, *Revelation*, 244; Fee, *Revelation*, 292.

27. Blount, *Revelation*, 378.

28. Richard Middleton, *A New Heaven and a New Earth: Reclaiming Biblical Eschatology* (Grand Rapids: Baker Academic, 2014), 205.

29. Middleton, *A New Heaven and a New Earth*, 206.

30. David Mathewson, *A New Heaven and a New Earth: The Meaning and Function of the Old Testament in Revelation 21.1 – 22.5*, JSNT Supplement Series 238 (London/New York: Sheffield Academic Press, 2003), 31; see also Richard Bauckham, *The Theology of the Book of Revelation* (Cambridge: Cambridge University Press, 1993), 132; and David E. Aune, *Revelation 17–22*, Word Biblical Commentary 52c (Grand Rapids: Zondervan, 1998), 443–457.

one, precisely because God himself is its architect and executor.[31] The apocalyptic visionary expresses God's sovereignty and "final say" in this "renewal event" when he draws on the concept of a great voice from the heavenly throne (21:3a) that announces God's dwelling or "tabernacling" among humankind (21:3b), an echo of the Johannine Logos's activity in John 1:14. If our author is drawing on the Jewish Scriptures, then he appears to reinterpret the concept of the tabernacle in Jewish thought that symbolized God's abiding presence among Israel (Exod 25:8). God's glorious presence could be experienced in the tabernacle (Exod 40:30–35) and, as Bauckham graphically puts it with reference to the text in Revelation, "The theo-centricity of Revelation . . . is focused again in the description of the New Jerusalem. God's creation reaches its eschatological fulfilment when it becomes the scene of God's immediate presence. This, in the last resort, is what is 'new' about the new creation. It is the old creation filled with God's presence."[32]

Consequently, the author of Revelation leaves no doubt that inhabitants of the New Jerusalem will be God's own people (21:3c). The author is thereby echoing God's promise to dwell with his people Israel and to be their God (Ezek 37:27–28; Zech 8:8) as well as to welcome other nations into the commonwealth of the redeemed (Isa 19:24–25; 56:6–8). Similar to Ezekiel's vision in 48:35, "The new Jerusalem becomes the perfect place for the gathering of the redeemed, a symbol of the long-awaited union of God and his faithful people. God's presence in the city will banish the things of the former order."[33] That being the case, Revelation 21:4 itemizes the removal of all that constitutes a threat to human existence or throws the ecology out of gear, including death, mourning, cries of distress, and pain. The prospects of a positively and radically transformed universe through God's initiative must have constituted an important eschatological hope for the author and addressees of Revelation.

---

31. Mathewson, *A New Heaven and a New Earth*, 34.

32. Bauckham, *Theology of the Book of Revelation*, 140. See also John N. Suggit, *Oecumenicus Commentary on the Apocalypse* (Washington, DC: Catholic University of America Press, 2006), 183.

33. Ranko Stefanovic, *Revelation of Jesus Christ: Commentary on the Book of Revelation* (Berrien Springs: Andrews University Press, 2009), 577–578.

John D. K. Ekem

Impact of Revelation 21:1–4 on the Ghanaian/African Terrain

In his groundbreaking work entitled *New Testament Eschatology in an African Background*,[34] John S. Mbiti wrestles with the subject of eschatology and its implications for the African concept of time. He draws on examples from his own Akamba society in Kenya and contends that "For the Akamba, Time is not an academic concern. It is simply a composition of events that have occurred, those which are taking place now and those which will immediately occur. What has not taken place or what is unlikely to occur in the immediate future, has no temporal meaning – it belongs to the reality of 'no-Time.'"[35] Mbiti subsequently argues that within Akamba communities, what really matters is the "Long Past" and the "Dynamic Present," and that the "Future," in a linear sense, is non-existent.[36] He applies this concept of time to his analysis of Revelation 21:1–4, drawing attention to its relevance for the prevailing sociopolitical, economic, and religious challenges on the African continent.[37] The significance of Mbiti's work lies in the question he raises regarding the tension between the linear concept of time that many Western societies are familiar with, and the cyclical dimension that influences the thought patterns of many non-Western societies, including sub-Saharan Africa. Precisely the question that arises is the extent to which futuristic eschatologies that apocalyptic material, including Revelation, seem to champion can resonate with the African context. With particular reference to our subject of investigation, we should query whether the concept of a new heaven and a new earth that Revelation 21:1–4 portrays should, in the African context, be accommodated within the confines of either a futuristic or a realized eschatology, or both. Admittedly, such a query does not lend itself to a simplistic response, given the multiple influences of Westernization, urbanization, and industrialization on traditional African communities. One can argue, nonetheless, that the persistence of traditional African religious worldviews, with their cyclical orientation to events, particularly in matters of holistic salvation, points to the resilience of realized eschatological inclinations on the

---

34. John S. Mbiti, *New Testament Eschatology in an African Background: A Study of the Encounter between New Testament Theology and African Traditional Concepts* (London: Oxford University Press, 1971).

35. Mbiti, *New Testament Eschatology*, 24.

36. Mbiti, 24.

37. Mbiti, 83–85.

African terrain. This can be illustrated with reference to the soteriologies and eschatologies of African Independent Churches (AICs). These churches are "protest movements" against the "over-Westernization" of European mission-founded churches in Africa, considering the fact that the latter could hardly satisfy the deep-seated needs of their African audiences. Whether we characterize them as "Zionist" or "faith-healing" churches, these AICs teach their members to look forward to a better land, sometimes referred to as a "New Jerusalem," where peace, prosperity, and righteousness prevail.[38]

In assessing the reception history and impact of the text on "receptor communities" in Africa, it is apposite to examine some mother-tongue translations that have shaped people's theologies. The key issue of vernacularization as a vehicle for theological creativity in Africa also comes to the fore:[39] the critical role of African mother-tongue Bible translations in shaping the future of African biblical scholarship has attracted much attention.[40] Here I will draw on two case studies from

38. Mbiti, 85. On the worldviews of these AICs, see also John S. Pobee and Gabriel Ositelu II, *African Initiatives in Christianity: The Growth, Gifts and Diversities of Indigenous African Churches* (Geneva: WCC Publications, 1998); and Thomas Oduro, *Christ Holy Church International: The Story of an African Independent Church* (Minneapolis: Lutheran University Press, 2007), 18–42.

39. For a good discussion of the subject matter, see Kwame Bediako, *Christianity in Africa: The Renewal of a Non-Western Religion* (Edinburgh: Edinburgh University Press, 1995), 59–74; Birgit Meyer, "Translating the Devil: An African Appropriation of Pietist Protestantism – The Case of the Peki Ewe in Southeastern Ghana, 1847–1992 (doctoral thesis, University of Amsterdam, 1995), 94–104; John D. K. Ekem, "Jacobus Capitein's Translation of 'The Lord's Prayer' into Mfantse: An Example of Creative Mother Tongue Hermeneutics," *Ghana Bulletin of Theology* 2 (2007): 66–79; Kwesi A. Dickson, *Theology in Africa* (London: Darton, Longman & Todd, 1984), 96–97; John S. Pobee, *Toward an African Theology* (Nashville: Abingdon, 1979). Edwin M. Yamauchi, *Africa and the Bible* (Grand Rapids: Baker Academic, 2004), 205–213, also touches on the thorny subject of Afrocentric biblical interpretation.

40. John D. K. Ekem, *Early Scriptures of the Gold Coast (Ghana): The Historical, Linguistic and Theological Settings of the Gã, Twi, Mfantse and Ewe Bibles* (Rome: Edizioni di Storia e Letteratura/Manchester: St Jerome Publishing, 2011), 156–157. See also two of Ekem's other publications: *Priesthood in Context: A Study of Priesthood in Some Christian and Primal Communities of Ghana and Its Relevance for Mother-Tongue Biblical Interpretation* (Accra: SonLife Press, 2009), 188–189; "Interpreting *ton arton hēmōn ton epiousion* in the Context of Ghanaian Mother-Tongue Hermeneutics," in *Postcolonial Perspectives in African Biblical Interpretations*, ed. Musa W. Dube et al. (Atlanta: Society of Biblical Literature, 2012), 317–327. See also Bernhard Y. Quarshie, "Doing Biblical Studies in the African Context: The Challenge of Mother-Tongue Scriptures," *Journal of African Christian Thought* 5 (2002): 4–14.

Ghana with which I am most familiar. My two case studies come from the Asante-Twi and Gã translations that I have had the privilege to supervise as Translation Consultant of the Bible Society of Ghana. The Asante-Twi and Gã communities are two major ethnic groups in Ghana, occupying the middle and part of the coastal belt of Ghana respectively. Asante-Twi and Gã are both tonal languages and belong to the Kwa subgroup of the wider Niger–Congo cluster of languages. Asante-Twi is the most widely spoken language in Ghana, occupying over 40 percent of the linguistic slot. Linguistically, it can also be classified as the dominant dialect of the wider Akan group of dialects spoken by over 60 percent of the Ghanaian population. This explains why I am using a translation from this dialect as a case study.

Revised Asante-Twi Bible Published in 2012 (Translation of Revelation 21:1–4)

Section Heading: *Ɔsoro foforɔ ne asase foforɔ* [A New Heaven and a New Earth]

1. *Na mehunu ɔsoro foforɔ ne asase foforɔ, na kane soro ne kane asase no atwam, na ɛpo nni hɔ bio* [And I saw a new heaven and a new earth, for the former heaven and the former earth have passed away, and the sea was no longer in existence].

2. *Na mehunu kuro kronkron, Yerusalem foforɔ, sɛ ɛfiri soro Nyankopɔn nkyɛn resiane, na wɔasiesie no sɛ ayefɔrɔ a wɔahyehyɛ no ama ne kunu* [And I saw the holy town, New Jerusalem, that it was descending from the presence of the God of heaven, and that it had been prepared as a bride richly adorned for her husband].

3. *Na metee nne kɛseɛ bi firi ahennwa no mu a ese: Hwɛ, Nyankopɔn ntomadan wɔ nnipa mu, na ɔbɛtena mu wɔ wɔn mu, na wɔayɛ ne man, na Onyankopɔn no ara ne wɔn bɛtena* [And I heard a loud voice from the royal stool saying: Look, God's tent is pitched among human beings, and he will dwell in the tent amongst them, so that they become his people, and God himself will dwell with them].

4. *Na ɔbɛpepa wɔn ani ase nisuo nyinaa. Na owuo nni hɔ bio, na awerɛhoɔ ne osu ne yea biara nni hɔ bio, ɛfiri sɛ kane nnooma no atwam* [And he will wipe away every tear from their eyes. And death shall

be no more, and there shall be no more sorrow or crying or pain, because the former things have passed away].

New Gã Bible Published in 2006 (Translation of Revelation 21:1–4)

1. *Ni mina ŋwɛi hee kɛ shikpɔŋ hee, ejaakɛ tsutsu ŋwɛi lɛ kɛ tsutsu shikpɔŋ lɛ eho etee, ni Ŋshɔ bɛ dɔŋŋ* [And I saw a new heaven and a new earth, because the former heaven and the former earth have passed away, and the sea was no more].

2. *Ni mina Maŋ Krɔŋkrɔŋ lɛ ni ji Yerusalem hee lɛ je Nyɔŋmɔ ŋɔɔ yɛ ŋwɛi miikpeleke shi, ni asaa lɛ ato tamɔ ayɛmforo ni awula lɛ ahã ewu* [And I saw the Holy Township, which is the New Jerusalem, coming down from God in heaven and made ready as a bride dressed for her husband].

3. *Ni minu gbee kpeteŋkple ko maŋtsɛ sei lɛ mli kɛɛ, "Naa, Nyɔŋmɔ shishilɛhe lɛ yɛ gbɔmɛi ateŋ, ni eeehi shi yɛ amɛteŋ ni amɛaatsɔ emaŋ, ni Nyɔŋmɔ dieŋtsɛ kɛ amɛ aaahi shi* [And I heard a great voice from the supreme royal paramount chair saying, "See, God's dwelling is among humans, and he will dwell in their midst and they shall be called his people, and God himself will dwell with them].

4. *Ni Nyɔŋmɔ aaatsumɔ amɛhiɛiaŋ yafonui fɛɛ. Gbele bɛ dɔŋŋ, ni nkɔmɔyeli loo blɔmɔ loo nɔnaa ko hu bɛ dɔŋŋ; ejaakɛ tsutsunii lɛ eho etee* [And God will wipe away every tear from their eyes. Death shall be no more, and deep worry or distress cry or suffering shall also be no more; because the previous things have passed away"].

These two mother-tongue translations from Ghana illustrate the technicalities of transferring thought from one language to another. This exercise becomes particularly challenging when attempts are made to repackage theological concepts for different receptor audiences. With reference to the apocalyptic text of Revelation 21:1–4, one needs to tread cautiously in navigating from a first-century CE crisis situation and its theological response aided by rhetorically loaded apocalyptic literary device, to twenty-first-century existential realities being experienced by some Ghanaian communities. In a typical sub-Saharan African community, where the forces of destruction via political oppression, economic mismanagement and exploitation, social marginalization, religious extremism, and intimidation that generate a culture of silence prevail, it is easy to connect with the concerns of oppressive structures and the prospects of the ultimate triumph of good over evil[41] with apocalyptic literature. That Revelation 21 and 22 have emerged as the *locus classicus* of an awaited new cosmos in which forces of negation are thoroughly done away with explains the high premium Ghanaian Christian circles place on them. Revelation 21:1–4 is often read and sung at funeral services as a beacon of hope and comfort for traumatized families and friends mourning the loss of loved ones. The majority of ministers/pastors view the texts in a literal sense and teach them accordingly to their audiences. Many are unaware of the historical and theological background to Revelation and some avoid preaching from it simply because they are unsure of what exactly it seeks to convey. A few opine that we should not be so engulfed in sociopolitical matters as to lose sight of our inheritance in the new earth that God will prepare for the righteous and called ones.

Coming back to our Ghanaian mother-tongue translations, it is interesting to observe how the nuances of Revelation 21:1–4 are captured for the Asante-Twi and Gã readerships respectively. First, the prospects of a new heaven and a new earth are viewed in both futuristic and realized eschatological terms such that what is anticipated in the distant future is also hoped for in the present and foreseeable future. The latter is in tandem with the Asante-Twi and Gã concepts of time that are more cyclical than linear. This can be illustrated with the Odwira festival of the Asante-Twi communities and the Homowo festival of Gã communities. Both festivals are occasions to reconnect with the departed members of the community who have attained ancestor status, reconcile with the living, and pray for the ancestors to be reincarnated in the yet-to-be-born. Such an ontological bond between the departed, the living, and the unborn resonates more with a cyclical view of life than with a linear hope for an "end time" characterized by the nullification of the past and present. This throws some interesting light on the portion of the Nicene Creed which states that "we look for the resurrection of the dead and the life of the world to come" that can be

---

41. Joseph Quayesi-Amakye, *Christology and Evil in Ghana: Towards a Pentecostal Public Theology* (Amsterdam/New York: Rodopi, 2013), 51–86.

considered as a fulfilled reality in traditional Ghanaian thought. Writing with reference to the Odwira festival, Frank Adams makes the following thought-provoking remarks: "The Odwira festival was seen as an 'uninterrupted story' where the past, present and future were united in the Asante historical and cultural experience . . . it was celebrated as a purposeful sequence of events, from defilement to purification and to renewal; from disintegration to integration; from past to future."[42]

In any case, since the "New Jerusalem" (Asante-Twi = *Yerusalem foforo*; Gã = *Yerusalem hee lɛ*) is coming down from God himself in order to assume divinely prepared "this-earthly" dimensions, it should be a welcome antidote to current imperfections within the constraints of human existence. Significantly, the Gã concept of "newness," translated as *hee lɛ*, connotes "divinely breathed radical renewal" and brings out more powerfully the transformation envisaged in Revelation 21:1–4. The Asante-Twi equivalent of *foforo*, though quite apposite, is semantically limited in this context, unless it is qualified with an intensifier pointing to its high quality. In future revisions, translators may consider adding the qualifier *paa* ("very"/"most") to *foforo* in order to achieve a similar effect. The comparison of this "New Jerusalem" with a bride adorned for her husband, which experience is highly cherished in Asante-Twi and Gã societies, reinforces the qualitative and innovative nature of such a divine initiative. The concept of "throne," translated into Asante-Twi and Gã as *ahennwa* and *maŋtsɛ sei lɛ* respectively, brings out the element of divine authority that effects positive changes in society for the common good. The Asante-Twi and Gã equivalents are considered as visible representations or shadows of ultimate divine authority. And that is all the more reason why occupants of royal stools/chairs must be people of integrity whose leadership brings good fortune to their communities. As a matter of fact, "royal stools" in Ghanaian traditional contexts symbolizes societal cohesion. If God is truly coming to dwell among human beings, as the Asante-Twi concept of *ntomadan* ("pitching of tent") strongly connotes, then all the forces that dehumanize us ought to disappear and God himself will take the initiative to alleviate our sufferings. In the African/Ghanaian context, we cannot confine this to "other-worldly" domains lest it lose its relevance for current concerns about human survival and ecological balance.

---

42. Frank Kwasi Adams, *Odwira and the Gospel: A Study of the Asante Odwira Festival and Its Siginificance for Christianity in Ghana* (Oxford: Regnum Books International, 2010), 201.

John D. K. Ekem

Toward an African Ecocentric Eschatology

As African theological educators, the challenges of material poverty, socioeconomic exploitation and marginalization, and religio-cultural bigotry constantly stare us in the face. These propel us to rethink the content of the theological education that we have received and are passing on to others. Our theological seminaries, Bible colleges, and university departments of religion and theology usually operate with syllabi that tend to expose students to theological impulses from the North Atlantic region. While these are not harmful in themselves, they carry the risk of producing theologians who are unresponsive to pertinent issues in Africa or, at best, view them with spectacles that may not necessarily address key African concerns. This is particularly the case with eschatological questions. Unfortunately, candidates who undergo training for ministry in churches and the wider community are ill-prepared to recontextualize the theologies they have been taught in the face of other existential realities within their constituencies of ministry. Amazingly, the average Ghanaian/African student of the Bible and theology tends to think futuristically in matters of eschatology, and there is often a myopic worldview of "a pie-in-the sky" soteriology that ignores present-day concerns.[43] Obviously, approaching the text of Revelation 21:1–4 from this perspective is bound to be other-worldly rather than this-worldly, for which reason extremist Gnostic as well as Platonic tendencies will threaten to gain the upper hand. Yet it can be argued from the rhetoric of Revelation that the apocalyptic author is drawing attention to a radical renewal of creation by a sovereign God who is not limited by time and space and whose rescue package embraces the entire ecology, including human beings.

Such a comprehensive soteriologically oriented eschatology is not alien to the New Testament documents, as can be attested from Romans 8:18–25; Ephesians 1:10; and Colossians 1:15–20.[44] This is a cosmic reconciliation, but unfortunately it is hardly prioritized in New Testament scholarship. The clarion call to think ecologically beyond

43. See Collium Banda, "Empowering Hope? Jürgen Moltmann's Eschatological Challenge to Ecclesiological Responses in the Zimbabwean Context of Poverty" (PhD diss., Stellenbosch University, March 2016), 47; Onesimus Ngundu, "Revelation," in *Africa Bible Commentary*, ed. Tokunboh Adeyemo (Nairobi: WordAlive Publishers, 2010), 1603.

44. For a thorough discussion, see John D. K. Ekem, *New Testament Concepts of Atonement in an African Pluralistic Setting* (Accra: SonLife Press, 2005), 71–77.

anthropocentric concerns is gaining increasing popularity in Africa, and theologians who focus on environmental ethics are drawing attention to issues of ecological balance that resonate well with the eschatology presented by the apocalyptic visionary in Revelation 21.[45] Mante, for instance, offers what he refers to as "Ontological Guidelines for an Eco-Theology," drawing on the philosophical–theological concept of "perichoresis" ("mutual interpenetration"). He argues very persuasively that for contemporary theology to be viable in Africa, it must move away from "A mechanistic view of nature. . . . Insist on the relationality of every entity to its environment. . . . Develop an anthropology with proper ecological perspective . . . . Incorporate salvation history within an ecological framework and, thereby, develop an ecologically-oriented salvation history."[46]

There is no doubt that our theologies will be positively revolutionized if we offer enough space to biblical interpretation that takes the ecology seriously. African reflections on eschatology should include the implications of apocalyptic theology for a balanced ecology as Revelation 21:1–4 champions. We cannot dispute the fact that the Bible is the most important source for African theologizing endeavors. Working diligently to make God's salvific purposes visibly expressed here on earth entails a holistic approach to soteriology and eschatology that should not be exclusively anthropocentric. Our approach ought to be ecocentric and deeply rooted in the agenda of the sovereign triune God. Of particular significance is the fact that questions of "eternity" in Johannine literature that includes Revelation are treated from a cyclical, rather than linear, perspective, because the sovereign God is the One who holds the past, present, and future, bringing them together in a relationship of mutual interdependence.

---

45. Joseph O. Y. Mante, *Africa: Theological and Philosophical Roots of Our Ecological Crisis* (Accra: SonLife Press, 2004); see also Ogbu U. Kalu, *Power, Poverty and Prayer: The Challenges of Poverty and Pluralism in African Christianity, 1960–1996* (Asmara: Africa World Press Inc., 2006), 75–98; Lloyd Timberlake, *Africa in Crisis: The Causes and Cures of Environmental Bankruptcy* (Philadelphia: New Society Publishers, 1986).

46. Mante, *Africa*, 138–139.

Concluding Remarks

This essay has attempted to explore the relevance of apocalyptic litera-ture as a key component of biblical eschatology for the African context. The case study from Revelation 21:1–4 has highlighted the subject mat-ter of radical renewal of creation, not its annihilation, by the sovereign God whose redeeming presence with humankind and the rest of crea-tion makes all things new. I have argued that the text serves as a *locus classicus* for a "Theology of Hope" for African communities in search of holistic salvation amidst the hydra-headed challenges confronting the continent. A key issue is the maintenance of cosmic equilibrium via an ecocentric eschatology that is firmly anchored in the triune God. The current state of affairs is beautifully summarized by Friesen: "John's vision for the kingdom of God and his Christ has not yet been realized. Perhaps he would be surprised to learn that it has taken so long or per-haps not. His text has nevertheless remained viable across millennia."[47] It is hoped that this essay will help stimulate further discussion on biblical eschatology and its accompanying apocalyptic theologies, using relevant tools from African biblical hermeneutics.

For Further Reading

Allen, Garrick K. *The Book of Revelation and Early Jewish Textual Culture.* Cam-bridge: Cambridge University Press, 2017.

Boesak, Allan A. *Comfort and Protest: The Apocalypse of John from a South African Perspective.* Eugene: Wipf & Stock, 2015.

Collins, John J. *The Oxford Handbook of Apocalyptic Literature.* Oxford: Oxford University Press, 2014.

Fiorenza, Elizabeth Schüssler. *The Book of Revelation: Justice and Judgement.* Minneapolis: Fortress, 1998.

Gallusz, Laszlo. *The Throne Motif in the Book of Revelation.* New York: Blooms-bury T&T Clark, 2013.

Glabach, Wilfried E. *Reclaiming the Book of Revelation: A Suggestion of New Read-ings in the Local Church.* New York: Peter Lang, 2007.

47. Friesen, *Imperial Cults and the Apocalypse of John*, 210.

Herms, Ronald. *An Apocalypse for the Church and for the World: The Narrative Function of Universal Language in the Book of Revelation.* New York: Walter de Gruyter, 2006.

Kiel, Micah D. *Apocalyptic Ecology: The Book of Revelation, the Earth and the Future.* Collegeville: Liturgical, 2017.

Lee, Pilchan. *The New Jerusalem in the Book of Revelation: A Study of Revelation.* Tübingen: Mohr Siebeck, 2001.

Smith, Julie M. *Apocalypse: Reading Revelation 21–22.* Provo: Neal A. Maxwell Institute for Religious Scholarship, 2016.

Stephens, Mark B. *Annihilation or Renewal? The Meaning and Function of New Creation in the Book of Revelation.* Tübingen: Mohr Siebeck, 2011.

Trafton, Joseph L. *Reading Revelation: A Literary and Theological Commentary.* Macon: Smyth & Helwys, 2012.

CHAPTER 4

From Dispensationalism to Theology of Hope: Latin American Perspectives on Eschatology

Alberto F. Roldán

ABSTRACT

In this chapter the author explains the development of eschatology in Latin American perspectives from the classic dispensationalism to the Theology of Hope of Jürgen Moltmann. The author analyzes the presence of eschatology in Spanish literature especially in the Church and Society in Latin America (ISAL) and in the Latin American Theological Fraternity (FTL). He also shows the contrast in eschatological visions between classic hymns and the new songs in evangelical churches.

Introduction

The importance of eschatology within the corpus of systematic theology is beyond doubt. The author of Hebrews states that "in these last days he has spoken to us by a Son" (Heb 1:1), and the Son of God, Jesus of Nazareth, has inaugurated the eschaton. The Nicene Creed affirms that Jesus Christ "will come again with glory to judge the living and the dead; and his kingdom will have no end." In spite of this, eschatology as a theological theme was almost absent from the consideration of many systematic theologies for many years, before seeing a resurgence of interest at the end of the nineteenth century and beginning of the twentieth through the influence of authors like Albert Schweitzer, Albrecht Ritschl, Johannes Weiss, and others.[1]

Protestant eschatologies – especially evangelical – have largely developed in relation to the concept of the "millennium," dividing into historical premillennialism, dispensational premillennialism, postmillennialism, and amillennialism.[2] Although dispensationalism strongly influenced Latin American evangelical churches in the twentieth century, since the middle of the century a change of perspective has emerged, partly because of the influence of several theological movements, including Church and Society in Latin America (ISAL), liberation theology, and the Latin American Theological Fraternity (LATF).

In this essay, we will first consider the difference between classic and progressive dispensationalism, an important distinction given their prominence in evangelical theology in Latin America. Second, we will survey a range of Spanish literature that engages with various perspectives on eschatology, including the significant influence of Jürgen Moltmann's *Theology of Hope*. Third, we will interpret the presence of eschatology in a sample of evangelical songs which offer an important glimpse of the grassroots perspective on eschatology in Latin America. Finally, we will respond to the question: How are the Nicene Creed's eschatological commitments present in Latin American theologies today?

Classic Dispensationalism and Progressive Dispensationalism

For much of the twentieth century, evangelical churches in Latin America were heavily influenced by dispensationalism. According to this theological stream, developed by the English theologian John Nelson Darby, one of the founders of the Plymouth Brethren movement, and based on a book written by the Jesuit Manuel Lacunza, the Bible must be interpreted in relation to different "dispensations" or "economies,"

---

1. For an analysis of the historical route of eschatology in the nineteenth and twentieth centuries, see Alberto F. Roldán, *Eschatology: An Integral Vision from Latin America* (*Escatología: Una Visión Integral desde América Latina*) (Buenos Aires: Ediciones Kairós, 2002), 19–56 (2nd rev. ed.: *Escatología: ¿Ciencia ficción o Reino de Dios?* [Buenos Aires: Ediciones Kairós, 2019]).

2. See Roldán, *Eschatology*, 89–114. For a panoramic view of the various views on the millennium, see Robert G. Clouse, ed., *The Meaning of the Millennium: Four Views* (Downers Grove: InterVarsity Press, 1977).

ways in which God deals with human beings. It distinguishes several dispensations or stages, and makes a strong separation between the Old Testament and the New Testament. In its classic version, the kingdom that Jesus of Nazareth offered to the Jews was the theocratic-Davidic kingdom, which, when rejected, led to the creation of the church, a reality not foreseen in the Old Testament. While Darby was the systematizer of dispensationalism, the instrument that popularized it was Scofield's Bible, translated late into Spanish but frequently read by English missionaries and then by pastors and believers who had access to it in that language.

The initial success of dispensationalism was due to the strong influence exercised by American fundamentalism and the fact that it constitutes a very complete scheme of the future of history and its eschatological culmination. From the 1960s, nuances in classic dispensationalism gradually modified some inflexible positions. The influence of theologians such as Dwight Pentecost and Charles Ryrie should be mentioned here.[3] Subsequently, a review of classic dispensationalism was made in the book *Progressive Dispensationalism* by Craig Blaising and Darrell Bock.[4] While highlighting broad commitments shared by all dispensational traditions, they advocated for "progressive dispensationalism," a perspective that "offers a number of modifications to classical and revised dispensationalism which brings dispensationalism to contemporary evangelical biblical interpretation."[5]

For Blaising and Bock, the most important aspects of classic dispensationalism are the following: the central dualism that recognizes two different purposes for Israel and the church; an emphasis on dispensations as different economies of God in his relationship with humanity; the heavenly nature of the church; the biblical covenants with Abraham, with Moses, and with Christ; and the difference between the kingdom of God and the kingdom of heaven. In contrast, progressive dispensationalism emphasizes holistic redemption and a progressive revelation; the nature of the church as a reality that exists in this dispensation prior to the second coming of Christ; the consistent and historical interpretation

---

3. J. Dwight Pentecost, *Things to Come: A Study in Biblical Eschatology* (Grand Rapids: Zondervan, 1958); Charles C. Ryrie, *Dispensationalism Today* (Chicago: Moody, 1965).

4. Craig A. Blaising and Darrell L. Bock, *Progressive Dispensationalism* (Grand Rapids: Baker, 1993).

5. Blaising and Bock, *Progressive Dispensationalism*, 22.

of the Bible; and the identification between the kingdom of God and the kingdom of heaven and the presence of this kingdom in our times.

Eschatology in Spanish Theological Literature

Dispensationalism has had a significant influence on Spanish theological literature on eschatology. For example, in *Eventos del Porvenir: Estudios de Escatología Bíblica* (*Things to Come: Studies of Biblical Eschatology*), Dwight Pentecost examines the hermeneutics of prophecy, covenants in the Bible, and the scriptural meaning of the millennium from a dispensationalist perspective.[6] Similarly, in *Dispensacionalismo, Hoy*, Charles Ryrie critiques covenant theology and explores the meaning of dispensations, the origin of dispensationalism, the hermeneutic of dispensationalism, salvation, the church, and the eschatology of dispensationalism.[7]

In addition to American authors whose works gained influence in the Latin American context, Latin American theologians have also advocated for the dispensationalist view. For example, Evis Carballosa is a Cuban theologian who represents the classic dispensationalist view. In *Cristo en el Milenio*, Carballosa offers an overview of what Christians should expect with regard to the millennium, and also criticizes the amillennial tendency to transpose millennial prophecies into generic descriptions of the eternal kingdom of God.[8]

The decline of dispensationalism in the mid-twentieth century was due in part to the popular influence of books such as Hal Lindsey's *The Late Great Planet Earth* which, drafted in the midst of the Cold War, posited the USSR as the great antichrist who had to be defeated. The collapse of real socialism and the disappearance of the Soviet Union quickly made this postulate outdated. Lindsey's work is a model of "science-fiction" eschatology. From a firm conviction of the "secret rapture" of the church and an interpretation of a series of current events – such as the formation of the European Economic Community and the Soviet

6. J. Dwight Pentecost, *Eventos del Porvenir: Estudios de Escatología Bíblica*, 2nd ed. (Miami: Editorial Vida, 1989; original: Grand Rapids: Zondervan, 1976).

7. Charles C. Ryrie, *Dispensacionalismo, Hoy*, trans. Evis Carballosa Tarrasa (Barcelona: Publicaciones Portavoz Evangélico, 1974; original: *Dispensationalism Today* [Chicago: Moody Bible Institute, 1965]).

8. Evis L. Carballosa, *Cristo en el Milenio: La Gloria del Rey de Reyes* (Grand Rapids: Publicaciones Portavoz Evangélico, 2007).

Union, which represented a perceived peril – Lindsey identified persons and movements as signs of a near end of the world.

Vendré Otra Vez, by George E. Ladd, represents historic premillennialism.[9] The theologian of Fuller Seminary considers the importance of Christian eschatology for the meaning of history. He discusses the second coming of Christ in contemporary theology, the biblical presuppositions, and the relationship between the second coming and the lordship of Christ. The conclusion of Ladd is that the parousia of Christ represents the final irruption of God in history and the consummation of redemption.

Anthony Hoekema's book *La Biblia y el Futuro*[10] is important for the amillennialist perspective. This is a complete exposition of the different perspectives on eschatology. Hoekema develops many aspects of biblical eschatology. He interprets the millennium from a symbolic perspective.

The Influence of the Theology of Hope in the Academic Environment

Church and Society in Latin America (ISAL)

Starting in the 1960s, three movements created important changes in the development of eschatology in Latin America. The first was the Church and Society in Latin America (ISAL: Iglesia y Sociedad en América Latina), which lasted from 1961 to 1971 and was the first Latin American Protestant movement devoted to social and political realities. Theologians such as José Míguez Bonino, Richard Shaull, and Rubem Alves considered eschatology to be an important subject. In an article written in 1964 entitled "Theological Foundations of Social Responsibility of the Church," Argentinian Methodist theologian Míguez Bonino exposits the theme by focusing on the kingdom of God and the lordship of Jesus Christ. About this last reality he notes that for both Luther and Calvin, Jesus Christ is Lord, although for the German Reformer there are two kingdoms. He adds: "Divine sovereignty in the totality of human

9. George Eldon Ladd, *Vendré Otra Vez*, trans. Edwin Sipowicz (Buenos Aires: Ediciones Certeza, 1973; original: *Jesus Christ and History* [Downers Grove: InterVarsity Christian Fellowship, 1963]).

10. Anthony A. Hoekema, *La Biblia y el futuro*, trans. Norberto E. Wolf (Grand Rapids: Subcomisión Literatura Cristiana, 1984).

reality, individually and socially, is also Calvin's point of departure."[11] To speak of sovereignty, moreover, is to speak of the kingdom and its relationship to the church. This leads Míguez Bonino to refer to the communal structure of the church as a prefiguration of the kingdom. Míguez Bonino criticizes the inversion of the biblical notion of the kingdom of God in Christianity through history. He posits that the dominant idea of the kingdom of God is an individualistic hope for immortal and celestial life but not for the transformation of the world.[12]

In those early works of ISAL, the Brazilian theologian Rubem Alves is the one who most emphasizes eschatology and the kingdom of God. In his chapter entitled "The Social Ministry of the Local Church," Alves interprets what the action of God consists of. From Jesus Christ we understand the action of God, whose purpose is to lead human history to its initial purpose: love and harmony. God acts dynamically in history by exterminating the powers that rebel against his love, and alters the historical order with chaos and disorder. What place has the kingdom of God in this approach? Alves argues that the kingdom of God represents God's sovereignty over all spheres of life and has radical projections on social and political structures.[13]

Another influential theologian in ISAL was Richard Shaull. In his book *Encounter of Revolution*, Shaull describes the presence of the kingdom in the world, affirming that "God broke into history in Jesus Christ and established His kingdom among men."[14] Shaull explains: "God was present in his kingdom, offering new possibilities of life to men and nations. Jesus healed the sick, fed the hungry, opened the eyes of the blind, and brought good news to the poor. . . . These acts were signs of a reality already present. The kingdom of God had come."[15]

Moreover, this kingdom looks toward a final fulfillment. The incarnation is the beginning but not the end of this kingdom. "We now live 'between the times,'" Shaul explains, and "between these two events,

---

11. José Míguez Bonino, "Fundamentos Teológicos de la Responsabilidad Social de la Iglesia," in *Responsabilidad social del cristiano*, ed. Rodolfo Obermüller et al. (Montevideo: ISAL, 1964), 25.

12. José Míguez Bonino, *Doing Theology in a Revolutionary Situation* (Philadelphia: Fortress, 1975), 133.

13. Rubem Alves, "El ministerio social de la iglesia local," in Obermüller, *Responsabilidad social del cristiano*, 57.

14. Richard Shaull, *Encounter of Revolution* (New York: Association Press, 1955), 50.

15. Shaull, *Encounter of Revolution*, 60.

and in this 'interim' God is at work. In it, history moves forward toward the goal which he has determined for it."[16] ISAL offered a new approach to eschatology in relation to the political and social situation in Latin America.

Latin American Theological Fraternity (LATF)

The topic of the second meeting held in Lima, Peru, by the Latin American Theological Fraternity (LATF, or FTL) was "the kingdom of God." Emilio Antonio Núñez talked about the nature of the kingdom of God. The Central American theologian distinguished two dimensions of the kingdom of God: vertical and horizontal; and he showed the immanent and transcendent character of the kingdom.[17]

Moreover, Núñez said, "The church reflects the tension between the 'now' and 'not yet' of the kingdom of God and out of the church it is not possible to think its existence. The church is the simultaneous affirmation of the kingdom of God as a present reality and as a future reality."[18] In Núñez's comments we can see a stark contrast with the dispensationalist theologies of earlier generations. In a similar vein, Samuel Escobar elucidates the negative consequences for social and political questions that sometimes accompany dispensational eschatologies: "A *dispensational* and *premillennial* theology assumes the vision of a fallen world whose sinfulness is reflected in its structures and ways of life. The kingdom of God will burst into the future. Therefore no kingdom of this world can be considered the kingdom of God. The consequence of this belief should be a critical attitude towards the kingdoms of this world and its opposition to the kingdom of God."[19]

Escobar's arguments stand in stark contrast to the vision of dispensational eschatology that was especially prevalent in the Pentecostal world. In this regard, Howard Snyder, citing Melvin Hodges, asserts that Pentecostals generally believe that the remedy for many of the evils of the earth is to expect the second coming of Christ. According to Hodges,

---

16. Shaull, 61.

17. Emilio Antonio Núñez, "La naturaleza del Reino de Dios," in *El Reino de Dios y América Latina*, ed. C. René Padilla et al. (El Paso: Casa Bautista de Publicaciones, 1975), 32.

18. Núñez, "La naturaleza del Reino de Dios," in *El Reino de Dios y América Latina*, 46.

19. Samuel Escobar, "El Reino de Dios, la Escatología y la Ética Social y Política en América Latina," in René Padilla, *El Reino de Dios y América latina*, 138. Original italics.

the return of Christ will solve all the social and political problems in the world. The only emphasis of mission is the transformation of persons through the proclamation of the gospel.[20]

Liberation Theology

Alongside dispensationalist, escapist eschatology on the one hand, and the politically and socially engaged eschatology of the ISAL and LATF, a third stream of thought came to impact evangelical eschatology in significant ways. Jürgen Moltmann published his *Theology of Hope* as a response to Ernst Bloch's *Das Prinzip Hoffnung*.[21] Moltmann reshapes the notion of eschatology from being merely a "doctrine of a future" to a "doctrine of hope." Moltmann shows the tension between futurist eschatology and present eschatology. He says: "'The end of all things,' it is said, must either lie wholly and entirely in the future, or have wholly and entirely already come, and thus be present. According to this viewpoint, future and present lie along the same temporal line. So it is also easy to find a reconciling solution when distinguishing in temporal terms between that which is 'now already' present and that which is 'not yet' present."[22] Moltmann thinks that this is an apparent solution.

Moltmann's theology was deeply influential, but was not without its critics. Rubem Alves, for example, first argues that his theology is essentially idealistic. "The pattern for the historical movement which Moltmann offers," Alves writes, "is . . . basically platonic. It is eros . . . which creates the *cor inquietum*. And more than that: God becomes the *primum movens*, as with Aristotle, pulling history to its future, but without being involved in history."[23]

Second, Alves criticizes Moltmann because he fails to do justice to the present reality of God. He says that the biblical communities "did

20. Melvin Hodges, "A Pentecostal's View of Mission Strategy," 88, cited in Howard Snyder, *La Comunidad del Rey*, 3rd ed. (Buenos Aires: Kairós, 2014), 71.

21. Jürgen Moltmann, *The Coming of God: Christian Eschatology*, trans. Margaret Kohl (Minneapolis: Fortress, 1996); Ernst Bloch, *Das Prinzip Hoffnung* (Frankfurt: Suhrkam Verlag, 1959).

22. Moltmann, *The Coming of God*, 6.

23. Rubem Alves, *Theology of Human Hope* (New York: World Publishing, 1969), 59. Cited in Timothy Gorringe, "Eschatology and Political Radicalism: The Example of Karl Barth and Jürgen Moltmann," in *God Will Be All in All: The Eschatology of Jürgen Moltmann*, ed. Richard Bauckham (Minneapolis: Fortress, 2001), 106.

not know a God whose essential nature was the future, the *primum movens* ahead of history. The Old and New Testaments speak about the historical present of God. The pure futuricity of God is a new form of Docetism in which God loses the present dimension and therefore becomes ahistorical."[24]

What is the difference between the theology of Moltmann and liberation theology (Teología de la liberación)? The central difference consists in the necessity to adopt political instruments to transform the world. José Míguez Bonino says that from his perspective, the imperative for today in the world is revolutionary action for the transformation of the structures and conditions of life in the economic, political, and cultural spheres.[25] For this Argentinean theologian, the transformation of Latin American societies will not come solely though the conversions of individuals, but through the adoption of political norms according to the paradigm of the kingdom of God. Míguez Bonino likewise argues that the Christian hope has its ultimate horizon in the *shalom* of the kingdom of God with the mediation of Jesus Christ.[26]

In general, American missionaries have adopted dispensational theology, but the theologians of Iglesia y Sociedad en América Latina (ISAL), Teología de la liberación (theology of liberation), and FTL (Latin American Theological Fraternity) have adopted the Theology of Hope. While the former is primarily futuristic in its eschatology, the Theology of Hope emphasizes one present eschatology to transform the world.

The Presence of Eschatology in Evangelical Songs[27]

The presence of eschatological issues in Latin American liturgical expressions deserves a detailed analysis that is not possible here. Nevertheless, we will examine several examples of hymns that might be called "classics" within evangelical hymnology, as their eschatological

24. Alves, *Theology of Human Hope*, 94. Cited in Gorringe, "Eschatology and Political Radicalism," 106.

25. José Míguez Bonino, *Christians and Marxists: The Mutual Challenge to Revolution* (Grand Rapids: Eerdmans, 1976), 7–8.

26. Míguez Bonino, *Christians and Marxists*, 111.

27. Some concepts in this section have been adapted from the chapter "La Escatología en la Teología Latinoamericana" ("Eschatology in Latin American Theology"), in Alberto F. Roldán, *Escatología: Una Visión Integral desde América Latina* (Buenos Aires: Kairós Ediciones, 2002).

emphases and perspectives stand in significant contrast to similar expressions in some songs in today's Latin American evangelical worship.

Consider, to begin with, the well-known hymn "When the Roll Is Called Up Yonder,"[28] which discusses the arrival of the "final day" in the presence of God:

1. When the trumpet of the Lord shall sound, and time shall be no more,
   And the morning breaks, eternal, bright and fair;
   When the saved of earth shall gather over on the other shore,
   And the roll is called up yonder, I'll be there.

   Refrain
   When the roll is called up yonder,
   When the roll is called up yonder,
   When the roll is called up yonder,
   When the roll is called up yonder, I'll be there.

2. On that bright and cloudless morning when the dead in Christ shall rise,
   And the glory of His resurrection share;
   When His chosen ones shall gather to their home beyond the skies,
   And the roll is called up yonder, I'll be there. [*Refrain*]

The emphasis of this hymn lies on the final judgment, and the author's poetry seems to be inspired by Revelation 20:11–15. The hymn says that "time shall be no more," but makes no reference to an intermediate period like the millennium on earth, before consummation. Although it speaks of "the saved of earth," which might be a reference to a corporate salvation, the whole emphasis is on the individual, as the refrain repeats "I'll be there." The phrase "home beyond the skies" seems to ignore the biblical perspective of a new earth. It does not appear on the horizon. As for the influence of this eschatological perspective on the present of Christians, it is reduced to "Let us labor for the Master" – not in terms of transforming the concrete, social world, but simply in talking about "His wondrous love and care."

28. Text and music: James M. Black, from *Himnario Bautista* (Buenos Aires: Casa Bautista de Publicaciones, 1978), 602.

We can also highlight the words of a hymn widely distributed in Central and South America, written by Felicia and Mariano Beltran and called "How Glorious Will Be That Great Morning":[29]

1. O how glorious will be that great morning
   When Christ Jesus will return to be adored.
   When the nations as sisters and as brothers
   Join to welcome the coming of the Lord.

   Refrain
   For the brilliance of that dawn
   Will outshine the brightest sun.
   All its heat and light give way
   To God's never-ending day.
   No more weeping will remain,
   No more grief and no more pain.
   For at last Jesus Christ, the Lamb of heaven
   'Throned in mercy, forevermore will reign!

2. How we wait for that great glorious morning
   When the God of love descends for us to greet;
   When the fragrance of Christ will bathe our senses
   In the rose light of dawn so rich and sweet. [*Refrain*]

Written within the same conceptual framework of the classic hymns already mentioned, this Central American poetry returns to the themes of heaven, the heavenly home, and the overcoming of anguish, crying, and pain in a poetic construction saturated with apocalyptic symbols. It affirms that in that heavenly place "the fragrance of Christ will bathe our senses / In the rose light of dawn so rich and sweet." Although all of that is true, it leaves parishioners with the question of how to solve the problems of the here and now, where everything is not "rosy." In other words, how can this future perspective help us to change the present state of things?

---

29. It appears as no. 549 of the hymnal *Celebremos Su Gloria* (*Let Us Celebrate His Glory*). The music of this hymn is by an unknown author, but with arrangements by Roberto Savage, copyright 1953, updated in 1981. The hymn as quoted above has been edited by professors of the Central American Theological Seminary of Guatemala and is dedicated, among others, to Guatemalan hymnologist Alfredo Colom Maldonado (1904–1971). Data provided by Professor Pablo Sosa of ISEDET. Translated into English by Mary Louise Bringle.

A very brief song, still sung in Pentecostal churches and, with ecclesiastical globalization, in many other renewal and neo-Pentecostal churches, is "I'm Going with Him." It says:

> Christ is coming, signs are there;
> Saved souls, He comes to seek.
> Those who slept will stay;
> Those who veiled, will go with Him.
> I go with Him, [x 3 times]
> I do not stay
> I go with Him.

In simple language, the author emphasizes what we have already seen in the classic eschatological hymns: the imminence of the "already," with a striking absence of the "not yet," and the fact that the signs have already been fulfilled to know that this is true. Christ comes to seek "saved souls," perhaps reflecting an implicit adoption of Greek dualism and the immortality of the soul, to the detriment of the resurrection of the body. With the expression "those who slept will stay," the song seems to adopt the strange hypothesis of a "partial rapture": when Christ returns, only those who are watching will be raptured. The ending emphasizes an individualistic profile: "I do not stay, I go with Him."

Finally, it is opportune to cite a different type of liturgical eschatology, one perhaps less pervasive than these others but nevertheless present, especially in the so-called historical churches. As an illustration, we mention "We Have Hope," a hymn written by the Argentine Methodist bishop Federico J. Pagura:[30]

> Because He entered into the world and into history,
> Because He broke the silence and the agony;
> Because He filled the earth with His glory,
> Because He was light in our cold night;
> Because He was born in a dark crib,
> Because He lived sowing love and life;
> Because He broke the hard hearts
> And lifted the despondent souls.

---

30. The music is by the Uruguayan composer Homero R. Perera and has a tango rhythm. Here the words are taken from *Cancionero Abierto* (*Open Hymnal*) (Buenos Aires: ISEDET, 1986), 66.

Refrain
That's why today we have hope;
That's why today we struggle with striving;
That's why today we look with confidence.
The future, in this land of mine.
That's why today we have hope;
That's why we strive with obstinacy;
That's why today we look with confidence,
To the future.

Because He attacked ambitious merchants
And denounced wickedness and hypocrisy;
Because He exalted the children and the women,
And rejected those who were proud . . .

Because a dawn saw His great victory
Over death, fear, lies,
Nothing can stop His story,
Nor the coming of His eternal Kingdom. [*Refrain*]

The mere reading of the words gives us the clear feeling that we are in the presence of a Christology and eschatology different from those exposed in the previous cases. The central theme is hope and, more precisely, the "why" of hope. It is a hope that is nourished and invigorated by the One who "entered into the world and into history." It summarizes the life of Jesus of Nazareth, his life of love and justice, his choice for the poor and the "downcast soul," and, as a counterpart, his criticism and denunciation of the "ambitious merchants" for their "wickedness and hypocrisy." Where does hope come from? It comes from both the history of Jesus and the eschatological future evident in the resurrection as a proleptic eschatological event ("a dawn saw His great victory over death") and in the blunt affirmation "Nothing can stop His story, nor the coming of His eternal Kingdom." Perhaps the refrain provides the hermeneutic key to understanding this eschatology: We look forward to "[t]he future, in this land of mine." The future of the triumph of Jesus Christ and the kingdom of God must be translated into "this earth," where we await the final consummation. It is, in short, the proposal of a dynamic hope, one which does not resign itself to failure but leads us to "strive with obstinacy."

Immersed in the world of image and sound, and abstracted by the force of music and participatory and emotional worship in churches –

aspects that are not negative themselves – we run the risk of not taking into account what is sung, that is, the theological content of the songs. There are no innocent liturgies, hymnologies, or aseptic songs. All songs respond to theological positions and doctrinal emphases, consciously or unconsciously assumed. The samples above have shown that, except in very honorable exceptions, there is a marked celestial and transcendent tendency in classic hymnology and evangelical songs. There is, in general, an assumption of the theory of the "rapture" of the church and an absence of hope for the world as a dynamic factor in the present. In summary, the eschatology expressed in Latin American liturgy is, in general, dualistic and spiritualistic, or has been directly replaced by other themes that have been instilled in the churches. It should be noted that this brief analysis of classic hymns and more current songs is not done to the detriment of the spiritual blessing and strength they may have provided in the past or continue to offer in the present. It is only a theological analysis of their content. What, then, would be an alternative eschatology of both the models of systematic eschatology and those expressed in the Latin American cult? An "integral eschatology" would offer an alternative in this regard.

Conclusion

The Nicene Creed affirms that God's "kingdom shall have no end" and "we look for the resurrection of the dead, and the life of the world to come." The question is, how are these affirmations present in the different schools of eschatology in Latin America? In classic dispensationalism, the kingdom is suspect because Israel rejected the gospel of the kingdom announced by Jesus Christ. All the dimensions of the kingdom of God are thus translated to the future: the millennium and the eternal kingdom. Progressive dispensationalism affirms the presence of the kingdom in the world now, but it is in the theologies of ISAL, the LATF, and liberation theology that we have the clearest, most systematic and most solid reflection on the kingdom of God. Under the clear influence of the Theology of Hope, Latin American theologians emphasize that it is necessary to transform the futuristic eschatology to an eschatology engaged with the here and now. The resurrection and the eternal life of the world to come must transform the present situations of injustice, poverty, and marginalization into justice, human dignity, and solidarity.

This is basically the perspective that the Nicene Creed offers to Latin American theologies. The affirmation "whose kingdom shall have no end" is present in the words of Federico Pagura: "Nothing can stop His story / Nor the coming of His eternal Kingdom."

For Further Reading

Hendriksen, William. *La Biblia, el más allá y el fin del mundo*. Grand Rapids: Libros Desafío, 1998.

Ladd, George E. *El Apocalipsis de Juan*. Miami: Caribe, 1978.

Míguez-Bonino, José. *Militancia política y ética cristiana*. Buenos Aires: Ediciones La Aurora, 2013.

Padilla, C. René, ed. *De la marginación al compromiso: Los evangélicos y la política en América Latina*. Buenos Aires: FTL, 1991.

Reyes-Mate, José-A. Zamora, ed. *Nuevas teologías políticas: Pablo de Tarso en la construcción de Occidente*. Barcelona: Anthropos, 2006.

Roldán, Alberto F. *Escatología: ¿Ciencia ficción o Reino de Dios?* 2nd ed. Buenos Aires: Kairós, 2019.

———. *Reino, política y misión*. Lima: Ediciones Puma, 2011.

Stam, Juan. *Apocalipsis*. 3 vols. Buenos Aires: Ediciones Kairós, 2003–2009.

CHAPTER 5

The Kingdom of God:
Latin American Biblical Reflections on Eschatology

NELSON R. MORALES FREDES

ABSTRACT

This chapter explores the eschatological concept of the kingdom of God from a Latin American perspective. The first section analyzes the eschatological perspectives of the Nicene Creed. A second section explores the relationship between God's kingdom and the doctrine of the church according to four important Latin American theological viewpoints (traditional Catholicism, liberation theology, the Latin American Theological Fraternity, and dispensationalism) and the way that each of these systems expresses the relationship between kingdom and church in its use of Mark 1:14–15. The study concludes with a consideration of the author's personal approach to the same passage.

Introduction

The 1970s and 1980s were tumultuous years in Latin America. In the midst of military dictatorships, Christians also made their presence known. In the circles where I grew up, there was a perception that Jesus's second coming was just around the corner. Prophecy conferences about the end times were common. We were taught to evangelize our neighborhoods in order to accelerate the coming of the millennial kingdom of Jesus. In other circles, ubiquitous poverty and systemic injustice were the concerns. How could we preach salvation without

confronting oppressive systems? The kingdom of God must be established here and now in order to eradicate oppression. Many thought
that the Nicaraguan political model of liberation was the example to
follow.[1] In Europe and the United States, the topic of the kingdom of
God was also under discussion.[2] However, the concerns were totally
different. Thus, the answers were different.[3]

Today, these distinct trends are still present in Latin America. After a
dialogue with the Nicaean-Constantinopolitan Creed regarding the present aspect of the kingdom of God, this chapter describes two external
influences on Latin American thinking regarding the kingdom of God:
traditional Catholicism and dispensationalism. It also presents two local approaches to the issue of the kingdom of God: liberation theology
and that of the Latin American Theological Fraternity (FTL). It will be
apparent that the way the kingdom of God is conceived affects one's
ecclesiology. Mark 1:14–15 is recurrently used in all of these approaches.
Consequently, after a brief description of the thoughts of each group,
an example of their interpretation of this passage is presented. After
describing the main interpretive trends in Latin America, I will briefly
develop my own contextual reading of the same passage.

Dialogue with the Nicaean-Constantinopolitan Creed

Given the importance of the Nicaean-Constantinopolitan Creed in
church history,[4] it is worthwhile to discuss briefly what it contributes

---

1. In 1979, the Sandinist movement managed to defeat the army and take control
of the country. Liberation theologians, both Catholic and Protestant, interpreted these
events as the establishment of the kingdom of God in Nicaragua. Antonio González,
"Reinado de Dios y signos de los tiempos," *Encuentro* (2004): 23–34; Ernesto Cardenal
Martínez, *La revolución perdida* (Managua: Anamá, 2013), 390–391.

2. See Christopher W. Morgan and Robert A. Peterson, eds., *The Kingdom of
God* (Wheaton: Crossway, 2012); Wendell Willis, ed., *The Kingdom of God in 20th-Century
Interpretation* (Peabody: Hendrikson, 1987).

3. See a detailed bibliography on the issue in Lesław Daniel Chrupcała, *The
Kingdom of God: A Bibliography of 20th Century Research*, October 26 (Jerusalem: Fran-
ciscan Printing Press, 2007); Lesław Daniel Chrupcała, "The Kingdom of God: A Bibliography of 20th Century Research. Update," https://www.academia.edu/33126266/
The_Kingdom_of_God_A_Bibliography_of_20th_Century_Research.

4. This Creed was formulated the first time in Nicaea in 325 CE, and later was
expanded in Constantinople in 381.

to our topic. As it turns out, the kingdom of God seems to have been a secondary issue in the elaboration of the Creed. At least, that is the impression received at the first reading. The eschatological aspects in the Nicaean-Constantinopolitan creed are mainly christological:

> I believe in one Lord Jesus Christ . . . who for us men, and for our salvation, came down from heaven, and was incarnate by the Holy Ghost of the Virgin Mary, and was made man; he was crucified for us under Pontius Pilate, and suffered, and was buried, and the third day he rose again, according to the Scriptures, and ascended into heaven, and sitteth on the right hand of the Father; from thence he shall come again, with glory, to judge the quick and the dead; whose kingdom shall have no end . . .[5]

The Nicaean-Constantinopolitan Creed focuses more on the "not yet" of the kingdom. In fact, the phrase "whose kingdom shall have no end" is located after mention of the judgment of the living and the dead. God the Father is explicitly presented as Creator of heaven and earth, not as King, although his kingship is implied in the imagery of the throne: "sitteth on the right hand of [God]." Except for this phrase, there is no mention of the current presence of Jesus's kingdom. The Holy Spirit is presented as Lord and life-giver who spoke through the prophets. There is no explicit mention of his empowering presence in believers. Finally, there is no explicit relationship between the "holy catholic and apostolic church" and Jesus's kingdom.

On the other hand, the "already" aspect of the kingdom could be derived from the Creed. In the fullness of time, Jesus the Messiah came to bring us salvation. Today, he shares God's throne. He is seated at the right hand of the Father. His kingdom will have no end. With his first coming, he inaugurated this kingdom. His ministry of salvation permitted us to enter this kingdom and be his disciples through our faith in him. The Holy Spirit is the life-giver of humanity.

---

5. Nicene Creed, as altered in 381, translated by Phillip Schaff, "English Versions of the Nicene Creed," Wikipedia, accessed 13 February 2019, https://en.wikipedia.org/wiki/ English_versions_of_the_Nicene_Creed.

Nelson R. Morales Fredes

The Kingdom of God in Latin American Eschatology

With this consideration of the Nicaean-Constantinopolitan Creed in the background, we will now consider ways that the relationship between the church and the kingdom of God has been addressed within four interpretive frameworks that have strongly influenced Latin American eschatology: traditional Catholicism, liberation theology, the Latin American Theological Fraternity, and dispensationalism. We will pay particular attention to the way that each of these views has interpreted Mark 1:14–15. After that, I will present my own reflection on the same passage.

Traditional Catholicism

Latin American Catholic eschatology develops along two fronts, representing traditional and more progressive theological concerns. The mainline Catholic front comes from Europe, through the direction of the doctrine of the church.[6] The second and more influential front has developed locally, through the writings of the liberation theologians. There is some overlap, but there are also strong differences. In both cases, God's kingdom is the central axis. This section presents the traditional view, and the next develops the concepts as presented in liberation theology.

Gabino Uribarri presents a good summary of the notable change in Catholic eschatology in the last century.[7] From the beginning of the twentieth century until the 1950s, Catholic eschatology had "a marked neo-scholastic orientation."[8] There was scarce dialogue with prominent topics in the Protestant discussions such as hope and the kingdom of

6. The writings of popes, councils, catechisms, and other official documents constitute the doctrine of the Catholic Church.

7. Gabino Uríbarri Bilbao, "La escatología cristiana en los albores del siglo XXI," *Estudios eclesiásticos* 79, no. 308 (2004): 3–28.

8. During the neo-scholastic era of Catholic thought in the second half of the nineteenth century, the eschatological topics, called the "newests" (*novísimos* in Spanish), were death, judgment hell, and glory. There was no discussion on the Christian hope and its relationship with the kingdom of God. During the first fifty years of the twentieth century, the Catholic discussion on eschatology revolved around these topics instead of on the kingdom of God and the related issues discussed widely in Protestant circles.

God reflected in the consequent eschatology of A. Schweitzer or the realized eschatology of C. H. Dodd.[9] During the years prior to the Second Vatican Council, there was growing consciousness about these themes of Protestant concern, such as the focus on life here and now instead of on the afterlife, the hermeneutic of eschatological statements in the Bible, an eschatology pertinent to the world and its problems, and the historical dimension of the kingdom of God. In particular, Catholic eschatology began to include the role of history and the world, and not just the hereafter. Studies in literature written during the Second Temple period, in particular that which related to the end of times, guided a revision of the Catholic hermeneutics of the *eschata*, the last things.[10] After the Second Vatican Council, the topic of God's kingdom became central for Catholic eschatology. Catholic theologians explored the eschatological tensions in the study of the historical Jesus and the Christ of the faith,[11] "their differences, their relationships, and their place in the life of the faith of the church."[12] There was reflection about hope centered in the kingdom. This hope had a historical aspect, without neglecting the hope in the resurrection. Cullman's expression became representative of the tension between the "already and the not yet" of the presence and implications of the kingdom.[13] The church is at the service of the kingdom of God, even though the difference between the two is not always crystal clear in Catholic literature.[14]

9. Uríbarri Bilbao, "La escatología cristiana en los albores del siglo XXI," 11–12.

10. Uríbarri Bilbao, 12–15.

11. With the quest for the historical Jesus, some scholars made a marked distinction between the man of Galilee behind the Gospels and the one drawn by the faith of the first Christians. That distinction was strong during those years after the Second Vatican Council – for example, in the works of authors associated to the Jesus Seminar. Today, many scholars recognize a closer relationship between the so-called historical Jesus and the Christ of the faith – for example, N. T. Wright, Craig Blomberg, and John P. Meier. The Gospels are a truthful testimony of the real Jesus. The Christ of the faith is the same Jesus of Nazareth.

12. Uríbarri Bilbao, "La escatología cristiana en los albores del siglo XXI," 16. In this and the following citations, the translations from Spanish to English are my own.

13. Uríbarri Bilbao, 15–17.

14. Uríbarri Bilbao, 17. Uríbarri points out that the church serves the kingdom of God, but is not equal to it. He quotes as a reference *Lumen Gentium* §5. But, as the next paragraph shows, the difference between the church and kingdom in that document is not so clear. The same happens with the discussion of the issue in *The Eschatological Character of the Church: Kingdom and Church in Select Themes of Ecclesiology* (1984) published by the Congregation for the Doctrine of the Faith, accessed 14 Feb-

A passage often mentioned regarding God's kingdom is Mark 1:14–15. In Mark's account of the beginning of Christ's ministry, Jesus announces the nearness of God's kingdom. By using these verses to support the foundation of the church, the Dogmatic Constitution on the Catholic Church, *Lumen Gentium*, seems to equate the kingdom of God with the church. The document asserts that even though this kingdom begins to manifest itself through the words, deeds, and presence of Christ, the church constitutes "the initial budding forth of that Kingdom."[15] Later, in 1979, the documents of the Third Latin American Episcopal Congress made this connection between the kingdom and church. Since then, the work and mission of the church have been interpreted as the mission of the kingdom. The Catholic Church is the sign, the visible aspect, of the kingdom. Its mission is to announce and establish the kingdom among all people.[16] The Catholic Catechism of 1992 uses the same verses of Mark to explain the foundation of the church.[17] Thus, in Mark 1:14–15, Jesus announces the kingdom of God and the beginning of his church at the same time. The church's mission and ministry is the mission of the kingdom. The church is the visible aspect of this kingdom.

---

ruary 2019, http://www.vatican.va/roman_curia/congregations/cfaith/cti_documents/rc_cti_1984_ecclesiologia_sp.html.

15. Catholic Church, "*Lumen Gentium*: Dogmatic Constitution on the Church," in *Vatican II Documents* (Vatican City: Libreria Editrice Vaticana, 2011), §5.

16. Conferencia Episcopal Latinoamericana, "La evangelización en el presente y en el futuro de América Latina," in *Documentos de Puebla: III Conferencia General del Episcopado Latinoamericano*, ed. Conferencia Episcopal Latinoamericana (Bogotá: Biblioteca Electronica Cristiana, 2008), §226–231. It will be apparent in the next section that the conclusions of the Third Latin American Episcopal Council were more in line with the thoughts of liberation theology regarding the role of the church as an agent of the kingdom than with the doctrine of the church represented by the thoughts of John Paul II and Benedict XVI.

17. Catholic Church, *Catechism of the Catholic Church* (Washington, DC: United States Catholic Conference, 2000), §541. The catechism adds that the church is "the Kingdom of Christ already present in mystery . . . on earth, it constitutes the seed and the beginning of this Kingdom" (§669). Pope John Paul II made the same point in his inaugural discourse at the Latin American Episcopal Conference celebrated in Puebla, Mexico, in 1979, against the more political view of the kingdom by the liberation theology wing of the Latin American Church. Juan Pablo II, "Discurso Inaugural pronunciado en el Seminario Palafoxiano de Puebla de los Ángeles, México," in *Documentos de Puebla: III Conferencia General del Episcopado Latinoamericano*, ed. Conferencia Episcopal Latinoamericana (Bogotá: Biblioteca Electrónica Cristiana, 2008), §1.8.

Liberation Theology

If the topic of the kingdom of God is important for the eschatology of traditional Catholicism, for liberation theology it is the theological center around which all other doctrines revolve.[18] The concept of the kingdom of God is viewed as a utopia, a path to walk in.[19] Liberation theology emphasizes the presence of this kingdom as an answer for those living in oppression and poverty. In the words of John Fuellenbach, "the intention of this theology is to recover the historical dimension of God's message and to move that message away from all abstract universalism so that the biblical message may be more responsive to the world of oppression and its social structures."[20] In this sense, their concept of the kingdom of God is linked to the historical reality.[21] The identification with the poor and oppressed in their time of need is a hallmark of true discipleship. In that vein, theological reflection is, according to Martínez-Olivieri, "a second act that presupposes a social location and

18. Jon Sobrino, "La centralidad del 'Reino de Dios' en la Teología de la Liberación," *Revista Latinoamericana de Teología* [RLT] 3, no. 9 (1986): 247–281; "La centralidad del reino de Dios anunciado por Jesús," *RLT* 23, no. 68 (2006): 135–160. See also Juan José Tamayo-Acosta, *Para comprender la escatología cristiana* (Navarra: Verbo Divino, 2008), 120–186. These thoughts are also present among Protestant theologians. See, for example, Mortimer Arias, "The Kingdom of God," *Westminster Theological Journal* 23 (1988): 33–45; José Míguez Bonino, "El reino de Dios y la historia: Reflexiones para una discusión del tema," in *El reino de Dios en América Latina*, ed. C. René Padilla (El Paso: CBP, 1975), 75–95; Elsa Tamez, "Poverty, the Poor, and the Option for the Poor: A Biblical Perspective," in *Option for the Poor in Christian Theology* (Notre Dame: University of Notre Dame Press, 2007), 41–54. Alberto Roldán focuses on this group of Protestant theologians in his chapter on Latin American eschatology in the present work. He highlights the thought of authors such as José Míguez Bonino, Richard Shaull, and Rubem Alves.

19. See, for example, Ignacio Ellacuría and Jon Sobrino, *Conceptos fundamentales de la teología de la liberación*, vol. 2 of *Mysterium Liberationis* (San Salvador: UCA editores, 1991); Sobrino, "La centralidad del 'Reino de Dios' en la Teología de la Liberación," 247–281; Jon Sobrino, *Jesucristo liberador* (San Salvador: UCA, 1991), 121–232; Jules A. Martínez-Olivieri, *A Visible Witness: Christology, Liberation, and Participation*, Emerging Scholars (Minneapolis: Fortress, 2016), 55–62.

20. John Fuellenbach, "The Kingdom of God in Latin American Liberation Theology," *Studia Missionalia* 46 (1997): 268.

21. Jon Sobrino emphasizes that "the theology reformulates and corrects the interpretation of the eschatological reserve as purely relativizing, and insists in that in history, it should be evident that truly it is God who reigns. And because the Kingdom is liberator, that kingship should be noticeable in all the levels in which slavery is present: physical, spiritual, personal, and social slavery." Sobrino, *Jesucristo liberador*, 223.

the commitment resulting from an encounter with Jesus in the lives of the poor."[22] The kingdom of God is present in history, so the church is an agent of the kingdom that brings and advances the presence of the kingdom by confronting oppression and liberating the poor. The fact is that the poor are the primary recipients of the kingdom. For that reason, the kingdom of God serves as the horizon where the church should focus its identity and mission.[23] As Sobrino emphasizes, "[the kingdom] enjoins that the mission of the Church be, like Jesus' own mission, good news to the poor, evangelism and prophetic denunciation, and the proclamation of the Word and historical fulfillment of Liberation. In this way, the church can be today a 'sacrament of salvation.'"[24]

Gustavo Gutiérrez explains Mark 1:14–15 from the perspective of liberation theology.[25] His explanation illustrates the centrality of the theme of the kingdom of God in the eschatology of liberation theology. Furthermore, this explanation reveals the close connection between liberation theology's concept of the kingdom of God and its ecclesiology. He introduces his analysis by highlighting the following: Mark anticipates that Jesus will face "resistance of the powerful of his time." He anticipates this by introducing Jesus's ministry just after John's incarceration. Gutiérrez connects Galilee with the ministry from the periphery, the borders. In Galilee, Jesus "recruits his closest disciples." "In the history that Jesus makes his own, the proclamation of the Kingdom is heard from the lips of those who are not listened to and who struggle for life and for recognition as human beings: the lips of the poor and the marginalized."[26] The proclamation announces the *kairos* of God, "a propitious moment, a favorable day, a time when the Lord becomes present and manifests himself."[27] The kingdom of God has come. God reveals himself in a special way in human history; his kingdom "is not something purely interior that occurs in the depths of our souls."[28] This kingdom inaugurated by Jesus "is present today in the person of Jesus

---

22. Martínez-Olivieri, *A Visible Witness*, 61.

23. Ignacio Ellacuría presents a clear argument for this thesis in Ignacio Ellacuría, *Conversión de la Iglesia al Reino de Dios: Para anunciarlo y realizarlo en la historia*, Presencia Teológica 18 (Santander: Sal Terrae, 1984).

24. Sobrino, "La centralidad del 'Reino de Dios' en la Teología de la Liberación," 277.

25. Gustavo Gutiérrez, "Mark 1:14–15," *Review and Expositor* 88 (1991): 427–431.

26. Gutiérrez, "Mark 1:14–15," 428.

27. Gutiérrez, 429.

28. Gutiérrez, 429.

the Messiah."[29] It is a dynamic reality, Gutiérrez comments, that gives to history its final meaning. "It implies a present development and has not yet attained to its full form."[30]

Jesus's announcement finishes with an invitation to repent and believe the gospel (Mark 1:15b). This is an invitation to enter the kingdom. It implies demands for certain kinds of behavior. Gutiérrez clarifies that "the acceptance finds expression both in thanksgiving to God and in deeds done for our brothers and sisters. It is in this dialectic that the meaning of the Kingdom emerges. The Kingdom requires us to change our present reality, reject the abuses of the powerful, and establish relationships that are fraternal and just. When we behave thus, we are accepting the gift of the Lord's presence."[31] At the same time, accepting the invitation is to reject the unjust world that oppresses the poor. It is to denounce the anti-kingdom. It is to proclaim liberation to the captives and good news to the poor (Luke 4:18–19). This example clearly illustrates the centrality of the theme of the kingdom of God in liberation theology's eschatology. This kingdom is not an abstract idea; it is a concrete expression of God's sovereignty in the real world which brings liberation to the oppressed.

Latin American Theological Fraternity

The Latin American Theological Fraternity (FTL, Fraternidad Teológica Latinoamericana) sees the kingdom of God as a central and unifying theme for eschatology.[32] Jesus introduces the kingdom with his person and ministry. "He is the Messiah in whom the Kingdom of God becomes

29. Gutiérrez, 429.
30. Gutiérrez, 430.
31. Gutiérrez, 430.
32. Juan Stam highlights that "the central theme and unifier of eschatology is the Kingdom of God. This theme dominates the Synoptic Gospels; in the Pauline epistles, it takes the form of the lordship of Christ, and Revelation emphatically reaffirms it with the triumph of 'the King of kings and the Lord of lords.'" Juan Stam, *Escatología bíblica y misión de la iglesia: Hasta el fin del tiempo y los fines de la tierra* (San José, Costa Rica: Semilla, 1999), 16. See also Valdir R. Steuernagel, "Forty-Five Years of the FTL and Its Biblical Theology: A Bit of Theology along the Way . . . and Mary," *Journal of Latin American Theology* 11, no. 2 (2016): 15–34; J. Daniel Salinas, *Taking up the Mantle: Latin American Evangelical Theology in the 20th Century*, Global Perspectives Series (Carlisle: Langham Global Library, 2017), 97–107.

a present reality. The church is the community that emerges as a result of his royal power."[33] Today, the kingdom of God continues acting in history through the work of the Holy Spirit. In this way, for the FTL, the triad kingdom of God, Holy Spirit, and church are intimately related. Padilla points out that "As a community of the Kingdom, the church is called to be, through the power of the Spirit, a new humanity in which love and justice, reconciliation and peace, solidarity and forgiveness, new attitudes and new relations take form. In other words, all of what signals the quality of life of the Kingdom [takes form] in the heart of history."[34] As a community of the kingdom, the church imitates its Lord in a holistic mission to the world.[35] "The historical mediation of the Kingdom is not a program but a community that lives by the power of the Spirit."[36] This community of the kingdom performs its mission nurtured by the hope of the fulfillment of the kingdom when Jesus comes again.[37] In this way, the eschatology of the FTL presents a more holistic view of the kingdom of God, one that takes into account the work of both the Spirit and the church. Not forgetting the future aspect of this kingdom, it considers its concrete presence in the world today.

A good example of this eschatology is the work of René Padilla. In his article "El reino de Dios y la historia en la teología latinoamericana" ("The Kingdom of God and History in Latin American Theology"), René Padilla deals with Mark 1:14–15. He explains that the kingdom of God is not just information about a future event but also a new order inaugurated by Jesus. God's dynamic power is visible through the signs

33. C. René Padilla, "La misión de la iglesia a la luz del reino de Dios," in *Al servicio del Reino en América Latina: Un compendio sobre la misión integral de la iglesia cristiana en Latinoamérica*, ed. Valdir R. Steuernagel (San José, Costa Rica: Visión Mundial, 1991), 21.

34. C. René Padilla, "El Reino de Dios y la historia en la teología latinoamericana," *Cuadernos deteología* 7 (1985): 11.

35. The holistic proclamation to all creation was the central topic of the Third Latin American Congress of Evangelization (CLADE III) in Quito, 1992. Fraternidad Teológica Latinoamericana, ed., *CLADE III: Tercer congreso latinoamericano de evangelización, Quito 1992; Todo el evangelio para todos los pueblos desde América Latina* (Buenos Aires: Fraternidad Teológica Latinoamericana, 1993).

36. René Padilla points out that this way of seeing the kingdom and the church avoids regarding both concepts as synonyms, and as a result having an ecclesiocentric vision of the Christian mission. At the same time, it also avoids the error of separating the church and the kingdom, turning the latter into a mere "historical project" without a concrete reality. Padilla, "El Reino de Dios," 12.

37. See, for example, C. René Padilla, *Mission between the Times: Essays on the Kingdom*, 2nd ed. (Carlisle: Langham Monographs, 2010).

Jesus does. These signs point to Jesus as the Messiah. This new reality has entered the course of history and affects "the human life not only morally and spiritually but also physically, psychologically, economically, socially, and politically."[38]

In this context, Padilla remarks, Jesus presents his message "the time is fulfilled, and the Kingdom of God is at hand; repent and believe in the gospel" (Mark 1:15, Padilla's translation). Paraphrasing Luke 7:22, Padilla insists that this message is not just a verbal message, separated from the signals that corroborate it; this message is "good news regarding something that can be heard and seen."[39] He derives five implications from Jesus's message: (1) it is about a historical fact that affects human life in all its dimensions; (2) it is of public interest – it has to do with all human history; (3) it is linked to the Old Testament prophecies; the *malkut Yhwh* (the kingdom of God) becomes a present reality; (4) it calls for repentance and faith; and (5) it results in the creation of a new community that recognizes Jesus as the Messiah and follows him.[40] In *Mission between the Times*, using the same passage, Padilla notes four facts with regard to the gospel: (1) "the gospel proclamation itself marks the *kairos*, the time assigned by God for the fulfillment of his purpose"; (2) "The content of the gospel is not a new theology or a new teaching about God but an event . . . the coming of the Kingdom"; (3) "The reference to both the Kingdom of God and the gospel points to Isaiah 52:7 . . . Jesus sees himself as the herald of a new age in which Isaiah's message – 'Your God reigns' – is fulfilled"; and (4) "the proclamation of the gospel is inseparable from a call to repentance and faith."[41]

At this point, some similarities and differences between liberation theology's and FTL's eschatology appear. The centrality of the kingdom of God in the eschatology of both currents of thought is clear. Furthermore, both of them share the view of a concrete presence of the kingdom in the real world of the needy. Perhaps the main difference is the role of the Holy Spirit. It is an important component in FTL's eschatology, but is almost absent in liberation theology's. In the same vein, FTL's approach is more holistic. It does not limit the current activity of the kingdom of God to just a physical/economical liberation; it includes

---

38. Padilla, "El Reino de Dios," 10–11.
39. Padilla, 11.
40. Padilla, 11.
41. Padilla, *Mission between the Times*, 87–88.

also the proclamation of the gospel of salvation and the spiritual needs of the people.

Dispensational Evangelicalism

An important segment of evangelicalism in Latin America considers itself to be dispensational. Alberto Roldán aptly summarizes the main theological distinctives of this system in his chapter on Latin American eschatology in the present book. Classic and revised dispensationalism is present mainly among Pentecostals and some other denominations, such as the Central American Mission and the Southern Baptists.[42] In their perspective, the kingdom of God tends to be circumscribed to a soteriological dimension (in the present) or is equal to the millennial/ Davidic kingdom (in the future).[43] The kingdom has a present component, defined as a rule or dominion.[44] However, even though today Jesus is King, he does not rule as a king. Jesus's kingdom is still future; it will begin with his second coming. During his earthly ministry, Jesus offered the kingdom; however, since Israel rejected it, the kingdom was postponed.[45] The church is not the kingdom but is included in it; it is

42. Currently, there are almost no influential Latin American theologians writing in these circles. The influence is mainly from North American works translated into Spanish. For a description of dispensational evangelicalism in Latin America, see Óscar A. Campos R., "The Mission of the Church and Kingdom of God in Latin America" (PhD diss., Dallas Theological Seminary, 2000), 95–147.

43. The Foursquare Church theologians Guy Duffield and Nathaniel Van Cleave comment regarding the present form of the kingdom of God: "The present (soteriological) Kingdom of Christ is spiritual and invisible, for it consists of the kingship, power and authority of Jesus as Savior and Destroyer of Satan." The future form of this kingdom is called "eschatological." Guy P. Duffield and Nathaniel M. Van Cleave, *Fundamentos de Teología Pentecostal* (San Dimas: Foursquare Media, 2006), 482. (Original: Guy P. Duffield and Nathaniel M. Van Cleave, *Foundations of Pentecostal Theology* [Los Angeles: LIFE Bible College, 1983], 445.)

44. Emilio A. Núñez, "La naturaleza del reino de Dios" (paper presented at the II Consulta de la Fraternidad Teológica Latinoamericana, Lima, Perú, 11–19 December 1972), 1–25.

45. The words of Charles Ryrie have been very influential: "Because the King was rejected, the messianic, Davidic Kingdom was (from a human viewpoint) postponed. Though He never ceases to be King and, of course, is King today as always, Christ is never designated as King of the church . . . Though Christ is a King today, He does not rule as King. This awaits His second coming. Then the Davidic Kingdom will be realized (Matt. 25:31; Rev. 19:15; 20). Then the Priest will sit on His throne, bringing to this earth

the agent of the present form of the kingdom.[46] In this scenario, the mission of the church is mainly to preach the gospel in order to hasten the coming of the kingdom.[47] Eschatology in these circles tends to focus on future events, on the "not-yet of the kingdom." There are some aspects of the present form of the kingdom, but usually they revolve around soteriology, as the following example illustrates.

Samuel Pérez Millos has written several commentaries from the dispensational perspective in the series Comentario Exegético al Texto Griego del Nuevo Testamento. Even though this author is a Spaniard, his works are influential in Latin America. In his discussion on Mark 1:14–15, Pérez Millos points out that "the gospel of God" is the message of salvation as a free gift from God. It proclaims to humankind the plan of salvation established from eternity.[48] He defines "kingdom of God" as "the sphere of God's government where God reigns as sovereign and is voluntarily obeyed." It is a spiritual government of God over regenerated people in the present time.[49] "The righteousness of the Kingdom is not external and ceremonial, but internal, from the heart."[50] Pérez Millos argues that in the phrase "the kingdom of God is near," Jesus is announcing the present aspect of the kingdom of God. In Jesus the Savior, the kingdom of God has come near to humanity.[51] Since this kingdom is eternal, it is present and eschatological at the same time. Those who accept the message of salvation enter the spiritual kingdom. Jesus's ministry opens the door to a time of divine fulfillment

---

the long-awaited Golden Age (Ps. 110)." Charles Caldwell Ryrie, *Basic Theology: A Popular Systemic Guide to Understanding Biblical Truth* (Chicago: Moody, 1999), 298.

46. Emilio A. Núñez, *Hacia una misionología evangélica latinoamericana* (Santa Fe: Comibam, 1997), 124.

47. See, for example, Campos R., "The Mission of the Church," 127–144.

48. Samuel Pérez Millos, *Marcos*, Comentario Exegético al Texto Griego del Nuevo Testamento (Barcelona: Clie, 2014), 128–129.

49. Pérez Millos, *Marcos*, 132.

50. Pérez Millos, 133.

51. For John D. Grassmick, Jesus's audience understood "the kingdom of God" as the messianic kingdom. What Jesus announced was "the governance of God is near." The kingdom was present in the sense that Jesus, the agent of God's government, was present among them. John D. Grassmick, "Marcos," in *Mateo, Marcos, Lucas*, El conocimiento bíblico: Un comentario expositivo Nuevo Testamento 1 (Puebla: ELA, 1996), 133. This series has been widely used among dispensationalists in Latin America.

and calls people to a personal encounter with God and himself.[52] The future aspect of that kingdom is the millennial kingdom that will end with the eternal kingdom.[53] Thus, as mentioned above, Pérez Millos's discussion illustrates that the present aspect of the kingdom of God is spiritual and focused on the salvation of the soul. The eschatology of dispensational evangelicalism is mainly focused on the future, and not so much on the present world.

In evaluating the four views presented here of the kingdom of God and its relationship with the church, the words of Benedict XVI are helpful. He summarizes the different interpretations of the kingdom of God in the history of the church under three main groups.[54] The first group sees the kingdom of God as synonymous with Jesus. As Origen called him, he is the *autobasileia* (the self-government). The dispensational approach appears to see the presence of the kingdom of God in this way, in particular due to the close association between Jesus and the land of Israel in this theological view. When Jesus was here, he was King. Currently, he is a king without a kingdom. He will have a kingdom after his second coming. Benedict XVI calls the second interpretive line "idealist." This way of conceiving the kingdom of God sees the activity of the kingdom inside the human being. The kingdom grows in and acts from there. This view seems to be the way both the traditional Catholic and the dispensational approach understand the present aspect of the kingdom. The third interpretive line sees different degrees of relationship and identification between the church and the kingdom of God. The approach of liberation theology appears to conceive of an indirect relationship between the church and the kingdom. The emphasis on the historical and political aspects of the kingdom and the poor as the main recipients of that kingdom tends to set the church aside as simply an agent of the kingdom. For its part, the FTL's understanding of the kingdom sees a closer relationship between the church and the kingdom. Just as in liberation theology, FTL's thinkers see the historical importance of the kingdom for today. For that reason,

52. Pérez Millos, *Marcos*, 134–135. Grassmick is more explicit in asserting that the phrase "the time has come" "emphasizes the distinctive note of fulfillment in Jesus' proclamation." Grassmick, "Marcos," 132.

53. Pérez Millos, *Marcos*, 133; Grassmick, "Marcos," 133.

54. Joseph Ratzinger, *Jesús de Nazaret: Primera parte, desde el Bautismo a la Transfiguración* (New York: Doubleday, 2007), 76–82 (*Jesus of Nazareth: From the Baptism in the Jordan to the Transfiguration* [London: Bloomsbury, 2008]).

they emphasize the holistic mission of the church. The Holy Spirit is the key factor in that mission. In this way, the FTL's conception of the kingdom of God is more Trinitarian.

Mark 1:14–15: A Latin American Reflection

Mark begins his narrative with a strong eschatological flavor.[55] In the prologue to the entire Gospel (1:1–15), the author introduces John the Baptist as the forerunner of the Messiah (1:1–8). In this way, the book begins with the New Exodus and the messenger of the Lord (Isa 40:1–5).[56] This connection between the Gospel and the metanarrative of the New Exodus frames the ministry of Jesus in the eschatological time of fulfillment.[57] Jesus is the one who will baptize people with the Holy Spirit (Mark 1:8). After Jesus's baptism, the Spirit who has come upon him leads Jesus into the desert and temptation (1:9–12). Jesus comes out from temptation in victory. The apocalyptic scene after the temptation arguably reinforces this eschatological framework (1:13).[58]

John the Baptist is reintroduced into the scene before Jesus's ministry (1:14). Now, the Baptist is in prison. The reasons for his imprisonment appear later in 6:14–29. Here the author uses John's situation to introduce Jesus's ministry of proclamation in a context of opposition,

55. I approach this from a literary perspective which accepts the text as it is. The relevant bibliography is considerable. See R. T. France, *The Gospel of Mark: A Commentary on the Greek Text*, New International Greek Testament Commentary (Grand Rapids: Eerdmans, 2002); Robert H. Gundry, *Mark: A Commentary on His Apology for the Cross, Chapters 1–8* (Grand Rapids: Eerdmans, 2004); Joel Marcus, *Mark 1–8: A New Translation with Introduction and Commentary*, Anchor Bible (New York: Doubleday, 2000); Joel Marcus, *Mark 9–16: A New Translation with Introduction and Commentary*, Anchor Bible (New York: Doubleday, 2009); Xabier Pikaza Ibarrondo, *Comentario al evangelio de Marcos* (Barcelona: Vida, 2012), Kindle ed.; Ben Witherington III, *The Gospel of Mark: A Socio-Rhetorical Commentary* (Grand Rapids: Eerdmans, 2001).

56. For more details on the use of the OT in this passage, see Rikki E. Watts, "Mark," in *Commentary on the New Testament Use of the Old Testament*, ed. G. K. Beale and D. A. Carson (Grand Rapids: Baker, 2007), 113–120.

57. Rikki Watts makes an important contribution to this topic. See Rikki E. Watts, *Isaiah's New Exodus and Mark*, Biblical Study Library (Grand Rapids: Baker, 2000).

58. See the brief and recent discussion about the eschatological imagery in Mark 1:13 in John Paul Heil, "Jesus with the Wild Animals in Mark 1:13," *Catholic Biblical Quarterly* 68 (2006): 63–78; Charles A. Gieschen, "Why Was Jesus with the Wild Beasts (Mark 1:13)?," *Concordia Theological Quarterly* 73 (2009): 77–80.

adversity, and evil. The forces of the anti-kingdom are already functioning. Jesus comes to the very region where John is prisoner. Galilee is central in the Gospel. Jesus begins and finishes his earthly ministry in Galilee (1:9, 14; 16:7).[59] Herod Antipas was the ruler of that region. So Jesus performs his early ministry among the people right at the lion's mouth (1:16, 21, 28, 39; 3:7). His proclamation is public, addressed to all the people.[60] In the same way, Jesus's disciples will face adversity and will develop their ministry in the midst of opposition (13:3–23).

Jesus's message is summarized as "the gospel of God" (1:14). Mark will show that this gospel from God is about the Messiah, the Son of God (1:1). In 1:14, Jesus continues the work that the forerunner anticipated. John prepared the way of the Lord by preaching repentance (1:4). Now Jesus announces the good news from God (1:14) and calls people to repent (1:15). His preaching is accompanied by doing miracles and confronting unclean spirits. Both actions bring health and deliverance to those in need (1:21 – 6:6). Later, as the Lord did, the Twelve preach the same call to repentance and bring health to the needy (6:12).

In verse 15, the evangelist presents the content of the gospel. First, Jesus proclaims that "the time has come." The time of eschatological fulfillment has arrived. In line with the New Exodus motif, Jesus the Messiah has appeared. He is the beloved Isaianic Servant upon whom the Spirit of God rests (Isa 42:1; Mark 1:11). The Holy Spirit guides and empowers him (Mark 1:12; 3:22–30). His disciples also receive the Holy Spirit.[61] In his power, they perform their ministry of proclamation

---

59. Fernando Méndez points out that of the twelve times Galilee is mentioned in Mark, five are in the first chapter. In this way, in Mark, Galilee is strongly linked to the beginning of Jesus's ministry. Méndez also highlights the fact that even the last two (of the twelve) mentions of Galilee relate to the beginning of the ministry of the risen Jesus. Fernando Méndez, *Marcos*, Comentario Bíblico Mundo Hispano 15 (El Paso: Mundo Hispano, 2012), 32.

60. Xabier Pikaza points out that Jesus did not stay in the desert – the place of the trial – nor did he go to Jerusalem besides the temple; rather, he went to Galilee, to his land and his people. Pikaza Ibarrondo, *Marcos*, Part 1, 1, "Necesidad humana y mensaje de Reino (1,14 – 3,6)."

61. In Mark, the presence of the Spirit leading the disciples in their ministry is implicit. In 1:8, the Baptist announces that one more powerful than he will baptize people with the Holy Spirit. In 3:13–19, Jesus sends the Twelve to preach and cast out demons. Immediately after, in 3:20–30, it is clear that Jesus casts out demons by the power and presence of the Holy Spirit. It could be inferred that his disciples cast out demons by the same Spirit. In Jesus's prophecies in 13:11, he exhorts his disciples to not be anxious when appearing before tribunals, because the Holy Spirit will speak

(1:7–8; 13:11). Furthermore, Jesus the Messiah announces that in this time of fulfillment, "the kingdom of God has come near." The Isaianic flavor of these first verses in Mark comes across strongly as Jesus echoes Isaiah 52:7 [LXX]: "Sion, your God will reign." The Servant of God is announcing the kingship of God. This eschatological flavor of Jesus's ministry is also present in his disciples' ministry (Mark 13:3–23). They should proclaim the same message until their Lord comes again (13:10, 24–27).

Even though, since the beginning, God sustains all his creation, he has burst into human history in the presence and ministry of Jesus the Messiah. Jesus's ministry is intimately related to the ministry of his disciples. In fact, immediately after presenting the summary of Jesus's proclamation in 1:14–15, Mark recounts Jesus's calling of the first group of disciples (1:16–20).[62] Since then, God's kingdom is present through the ministry of Jesus's disciples. Jesus sent out his twelve disciples with the same message (3:13–15; 6:12). Later, with the help of the Holy Spirit, they will continue their ministry in the midst of adversity and opposition as their Lord did (13:9–11). This kingdom also waits for a final fulfillment when the Son of Man comes with glory and power (13:26–27). The certainty of this coming gives hope to his disciples today.

This good news demands an answer from those who hear it. Jesus says, "Repent and believe in the gospel." This call to repentance implies several things: it implies sins from which to repent and people who must repent. Those who repent will follow the path of the Messiah by believing in the gospel. The rich young man is an example of someone who did not want to repent of his love of money. As a result, he could not enter the kingdom of God (10:17–31). He is like the seed among thorns (4:19). Other people accepted Jesus's invitation immediately and followed him (1:16–20; 2:13–14). They are like the seed in good soil: those who hear the word of the kingdom and embrace it (4:20). Darío López reminds us that, "due to individual, social, and structural sin, human beings act egotistically, looking to their own interests, without any regard for the wellbeing of their neighbors."[63] Thus, our proclamation

---

through them. Thus, in one point of the narrative, the disciples are baptized with the Holy Spirit. It is Luke who lets us know the moment (Acts 2), but in Mark it is implicit.

62. Osvaldo Vena rightly points out: "Like John, Jesus will need disciples to do his work. For that reason, his ministry does not begin without first calling his first collaborators." Osvaldo D. Vena, *Evangelio de Marcos*, CET (Miami: Sociedades Bíblicas Unidas, 2008), 29.

63. Darío López R., *La propuesta política del Reino de Dios* (Lima: Puma, 2009), 88.

of the gospel should not leave out the call for repentance. It should also include a denunciation of the social and structural sins less perceived by many Christian communities. In this sense, repentance is a key for entering the kingdom, but perseverance is also a signal of true discipleship. A disciple repents of his or her own sins, but must learn to live in a world under the control of the anti-kingdom. True disciples repent of sin, enter the kingdom of God, and bring the new reality of the kingdom into their world.

The church is the community of Jesus's disciples. As such, it is called to proclaim the gospel of God. As René Padilla says, "the mission of the Church is an extension of Jesus's mission."[64] We are still waiting for the coming of our Lord. In the meantime, with the power of the Spirit, we proclaim the good news of salvation. As Núñez comments, "God wants to bless all human beings and the whole human being."[65] So this good news also implies bringing help to those in need. This ministry is a visible expression that the kingdom of God is here. In Jesus's ministry, miracles demonstrate his mercy (Mark 6:34). They are not mere bait for evangelistic purposes. Evangelistic activities combined with donations of food or medical support have been common in Latin America. Often, in order for people to receive food, medical supplies, or attention, they are first required to hear the "gospel" and "accept Jesus." In this way, the help turns into mere bait for evangelistic purposes. Instead, the church's mission of proclamation should be accompanied by deeds of mercy. In this regard, Padilla points out, "[the church] is the manifestation (though not yet complete) of the Kingdom of God, through proclamation as well as through social service and action. The apostolic witness continues to be the Spirit's witness to Jesus Christ as Lord through the church."[66]

Thankfully, in Latin America, the practice of using deeds of mercy in their evangelistic efforts as a way to attract converts has declined over the past decade, but it is still a problem. Catholic works of mercy have set a good example showing that a more balanced ministry is possible. Also, many evangelical churches have developed a more integral work among their neighborhoods and in places of greater need. A very good example is the research which Claudia Dary presents in her book. It is a study and compilation of the work of several churches located in extremely violent neighborhoods in Guatemala City. The book shows

---

64. Padilla, *Mission between the Times*, 205.
65. Núñez, *Hacia una misionología evangélica latinoamericana*, 142.
66. Padilla, *Mission between the Times*, 205.

how pastors and churches, priests and parishes are fully involved in rescuing youth from the arms of gangs, with holistic ministries.[67]

The kingdom came before the first disciples of Jesus entered it. So the kingdom of God is not the community of disciples, but it includes them. The kingdom of God includes at least the redeemed creation, believers in God from Adam to the last one, and the holy angels. The church – just as its Lord was – is the herald of the gospel of God. However, there is an anti-kingdom force that opposes this ministry. In Mark, Satan and the unclean spirits continually opposed Jesus. Jesus also faced the religious and political establishment. In the same way, as agents of this kingdom, we should be a light that shines in the darkness of the world system that is utterly opposed to his kingdom and its values.

Conclusion

The eschatological concept of the kingdom of God has long occupied the agenda of Latin American reflection. The concerns have revolved around the presence of the kingdom today. Even though the concept is almost absent from the Nicaean-Constantinopolitan Creed, it has been a focus of wide and deep discussion in Latin America. Different approaches have emphasized different aspects of that presence. Dispensational circles have tended to see an absence of the kingdom. That absence has motivated them in their evangelization. For its part, the traditional Catholic Church has centered its focus on the inner presence of that kingdom: church and kingdom are so closely related that it is hard to differentiate between them. In liberation theology, the emphasis lies on the historical and political presence of the kingdom of God. The poor are the main recipients of that kingdom. In this context, the church is an agent of the kingdom and its mission is to bring the kingdom to the oppressed. The FTL presents a more Trinitarian approach to the concept. The church is an agent of the kingdom. Through the empowering presence of the Spirit, and as servants of the Lord Jesus, the church proclaims the gospel of God that brings help to those in need.

The summary of Jesus's proclamation of the gospel of God in Mark 1:14–15 is a good example of these different approaches. Jesus has in-

---

67. Claudia Dary, *Cristianos en un país violento: Respuestas de las iglesias frente a la violencia en dos colonias del área metropolitana de Guatemala* (Guatemala City: Universidad de San Carlos de Guatemala, 2016).

augurated the eschaton with his presence and ministry. The kingdom of God is present and manifest today through the ministry of Jesus's disciples who are empowered by the presence of the Holy Spirit. That same good news announces the victory of God over the forces that oppose his kingship. This victory will be definitive when Jesus comes in glory and power. Then God will manifest his kingdom in all its splendor, and all peoples will praise him.

For Further Reading

Martínez-Olivieri, Jules A. *A Visible Witness: Christology, Liberation, and Participation.* Emerging Scholars. Minneapolis: Fortress, 2016.

Padilla, C. René. *Mission between the Times: Essays on the Kingdom.* 2nd ed. Carlisle: Langham Monographs, 2010.

Roldán, F. Alberto. *Reino, política y misión: Sus relaciones en perspectiva latinoamericana.* Lima: Puma, 2011.

Salinas, J. Daniel. *Taking up the Mantle: Latin American Evangelical Theology in the 20th Century.* Global Perspectives Series. Carlisle: Langham Global Library, 2017.

Stam, Juan. *Escatología bíblica y misión de la iglesia: Hasta el fin del tiempo y los fines de la tierra.* San José: Semilla, 1999.

Tamayo-Acosta, Juan José. *Para comprender la escatología cristiana.* Navarra: Verbo Divino, 2008.

CHAPTER 6

Asia and God's Cruciform Eschatological Reign

ALDRIN PEÑAMORA

ABSTRACT

Eschatology plays a crucial role in the way Christians in Asia engage with issues of public or social-political relevance. While the principle of *Sola Scriptura* continues to be one of the bedrocks of Asian Protestant Christianity, historical and cultural factors have powerfully shaped it, as exemplified in Korea and China. Sadly, the eschatology that has resulted with the intertwining of history, culture, and Scripture has often led to little or no involvement of Christians in public spaces. This essay seeks to address this issue for the Christian community in order that it might reflect Jesus's cruciform eschatology that confronted the oppressions of his day in light of the dawning of God's eschatological reign. A proper resolution of this issue is of vital importance for Christians in Asia, where poverty, exclusion, and oppression have for so long been constant and deadly companions of the people.

Introduction

"From first to last," according to Jürgen Moltmann, "Christianity is eschatology, is hope, forward looking and forward moving, and therefore also revolutionizing and transforming the present."[1] In Asia, where multitudes of people groups have long been struggling against poverty and oppression, the Christian message about God's restoration

1. Jürgen Moltmann, *Theology of Hope* (New York: Harper & Row, 1965), 16.

of all creation can provide them with much-needed hope in their specific contexts.

Indeed, like all other Christian doctrines, eschatology is contextual. This essay will look at how eschatology, especially premillennialism, was appropriated contextually by the early Korean Presbyterian Church, David Yonggi Cho and the Yoido Full Gospel Church, China's "Back to Jerusalem Movement," and Watchman Nee and the Little Flock church. By presenting and examining the contours of their eschatological views, this essay aims to advance some critical theological insights that will hopefully be of some relevance toward addressing concretely the situations of the poor in Asia.

The Many Faces of Asia

The diversity of Asia's ethnic groups, histories, cultures, religious traditions, and political systems reflects the pluriformity of Asia. The notion that Asia is one was from antiquity one of convenience, which was firmly established when the world was divided into several continents during medieval times.[2] After World War II, attempts to conceptualize the oneness of Asia in political terms were not lacking, although the underpinnings and goals of those attempts led to contested visions – imperialist, nationalist, regionalist, and the like – that only strengthened the claim to Asia's many-ness.[3] Similarly, even with the notion of Christianity in Asia, an essentialist view of "Christianity" may refer aptly to a unity of basic Christian beliefs in contrast to other Asian faith traditions, but viewed historically the varied and frenzied ways these beliefs and practices have been socially embodied, expressed, and understood make the plural "Christianities" an equally appropriate designation.[4]

For Asia has always been many, with multiple conceptions that draw on various sources, such as interdependence, economic growth, ideational and religious foundations, and other material factors that in

2. Atola Longkumer, "Together towards Life and Contemporary Asian Theology," in *Ecumenical Missiology: Changing Landscapes and New Concepts of Mission*, ed. Kenneth R. Ross et al. (Oxford: Regnum, 2016), 499.

3. Amitav Acharya, "Asia Is Not One," *The Journal of Asian Studies* 69, no. 4 (Nov. 2010): 1002–1003.

4. Peter C. Phan, ed., *Christianities in Asia* (Chichester: John Wiley & Sons, 2007), 1–2.

different ways have contributed toward shaping the lives and destinies of peoples and nations.[5] It is this pluriformity that obliges the church in Asia to abandon absolutizing claims regarding a particular form of – or way of doing – theology. To insist on such runs the risk of once again expressing colonial tendencies of "intellectual, cultural, sociological, economic and religious imperialism."[6] Aloysius Pieris makes the important point that in Asia many metacosmic religions, such as Confucianism in China and Shinto worship in Japan, took deep root in societies centuries before Christianity arrived. These cannot easily be dislodged by another metacosmic faith, "except by protracted use of coercion – that is, by an irreligious resort to mass conversion."[7]

Poverty and religious plurality are key features of the Asian soil. According to the 6th Christian Conference of Asia that was held back in 1977, the "dominant reality of Asian suffering is that people are wasted: Wasted by hunger, torture, deprivation of rights, . . . by economic exploitation, racial and ethnic discrimination, sexual suppression, nonrelation, non-community."[8] Today, even with China – and India poised to soon rise – as a superpower, and the influence of other highly developed economies such as Japan, Singapore, and Taiwan, massive poverty is still prevalent in Asia.

Poverty and oppression in Asia, as Peter C. Phan remarks, is forced and imposed.[9] Historically, it is one of the unhappy and lasting legacies of past and often multiple iterations of political, economic, social, and religious colonization from the West, going all the way back to the arrival in India of Portuguese explorer Vasco de Gama. But while one may easily think of Asia's domination by Western powers, it is important to note that Asian powers themselves, like Japan, at one time or another also advanced colonial interests, and that Asian despots and

5. Acharya, "Asia Is Not One," 1001.

6. Engelbert Mveng, quoted in Frank Chikane, "EATWOT and Third World Theologies: An Evaluation of the Past and the Present," in *Third World Theologies: Commonalities and Divergences* (Maryknoll: Orbis, 1990), 150–152.

7. Aloysius Pieris, *An Asian Theology of Liberation* (Maryknoll: Orbis, 1988), 55. Pieris defines metacosmic faith as postulating the existence of "a transphenomenal Reality immanently operative in the cosmos and soteriologically available within the human person either through *agape* (redeeming love) or through *gnosis* (redeeming knowledge)." Jewish and Christian faiths represent the agapaic while the monastic faiths of Hinduism, Buddhism, and Taoism the gnostic (54).

8. Quoted in C. S. Song, *Theology from the Womb of Asia* (Maryknoll: Orbis, 1986), 187.

9. Peter C. Phan, "Jesus Christ with an Asian Face," *Theological Studies* 57 (1997): 401.

regimes have perpetuated oppressive measures toward Asian subalterns and minoritized citizens because of class (e.g., the Hindu caste system of India), gender (e.g., women), and religion (e.g., Rohingya Muslims in Buddhist-majority Myanmar).[10]

A second thread that connects Asia is the peoples' deep religiosity. As the cradle of the world's major religious traditions, in Asia religion is intertwined with daily life and with the very identity of the people. This is exemplified by the Moros,[11] or Muslims, of Southern Philippines, who consider religious identity to be of utmost importance as citizens of the nation. This aspiration to be recognized as Muslims is at the core of the longstanding conflict in Mindanao.[12]

Religious identity or affiliation is thus often invoked in armed struggles in Asia.[13] Undeniably, many violent conflicts contain religious elements. However, we would be amiss to view religion and violence as intrinsically intertwined. "The idea that religion causes violence," as William Cavanaugh incisively points out, "is one of the most prevalent myths in Western culture."[14] Many elements usually converge to enable

10. See Phan, "Jesus Christ with an Asian Face," 401. K. M. Panikkar calls the period of Western colonization of Asia the "de Gama epoch," which started from the Portuguese explorer's arrival in India in 1498 and lasted until the end of World War II in 1945. It is a period that is unified by these four features: (1) the dominance of the maritime power of Asia's landmasses; (2) the imposition of an economic life based not on the usual agricultural economy but on international trade; (3) the domination of Europeans over the affairs of Asia; and (4) attempts by Europeans to Christianize Asia. K. M. Panikkar, *Asia and Western Dominance: A Survey of the Vasco de Gama Epoch of Asian History 1498–1945* (London: George Allen & Unwin, 1959), 13–15.

11. From the word "Moors," the term "Moro" was used derogatorily by the Spanish colonizers to refer to the Muslims of Mindanao, Sulu, and Palawan in Southern Philippines.

12. At the present time, representing the Moro people in their struggle for meaningful self-determination is the Moro Islamic Liberation Front (MILF). Their demand for genuine self-determination is encapsulated in the "Bangsamoro Organic Law" (BOL) that was signed into law on 26 July 2018.

13. Bardwell L. Smith, "Religion, Social Conflict and the Problem of Identity in South Asia: An Interpretive Introduction," in *Religion and Social Conflict in South Asia*, ed. Bardwell L. Smith (Leiden: Brill, 1976), 7.

14. William T. Cavanaugh, *The Myth of Religious Violence: Secular Ideology and the Roots of Modern Conflict* (Oxford: Oxford University Press, 2009), 15. On pages 181–183, Cavanaugh points out various ways in which the myth of religious violence is a useful construct for the West, particularly in reinforcing power in domestic and foreign politics. Although not without many critics, Edward Said put forth a similar notion, arguing that the concept of "Oriental" was conjured by the West for its own purposes.

violence and armed insurgencies.[15] Indeed, religious symbols, principles, and doctrines have been utilized for various ends that include radical and violent ones.[16] Nonetheless, Asian religions also play a vital role in bringing peace and protesting abuses in society. The Indian independence movement of Mahatma Gandhi and the Philippine "People Power" that brought down a dictator are fine examples. But as conflicts proliferate in religiously pluralistic Asia, conflicts which are increasingly being defined as clashes of civilizations, Phan is correct to observe that they "cannot be resolved without the harmony of religions."[17]

Contextual Eschatology in Asia

With the end of World War II, the de Gama epoch came to an end. Song called this a *kairotic* year, a year that did not just affect drastically the lives of countless peoples in Asia, but which enabled history to be intelligible and to have meaning. From the ashes of war arose nations that were at long last free – or at least relatively free.[18] In the following we

---

He writes, "Orientalism can be discussed and analyzed as the corporate institution for dealing with the Orient – dealing with it by making statements about it, authorizing views of it, describing it, by teaching it, settling it, ruling over it: in short, Orientalism as a Western style for dominating, restructuring, and having authority over the Orient" (*Orientalism: Western Conceptions of the Orient* [London: Routledge, 1978], 3).

15. William Gould, *Religion and Conflict in Modern South Asia* (Cambridge: Cambridge University Press, 2012), 309. Gould further makes the point that South Asia should not be defined mainly in relation to religious traditions. The civil war in Sri Lanka, for instance, between the Sinhalese Buddhists and Tamil Muslims, can be viewed superficially as a clash of religions, but, on closer examination, contributing factors include international, domestic, socioeconomic, and religio-cultural matters. He ultimately concludes that it is primarily an "ethnonationalist insurgency wherein various communities defined themselves and their antagonists by ethnicity and faith tradition." Berkeley Center for Religion, Peace and World Affairs, *Civil War along Ethnoreligious Lines* (Washington DC: Georgetown University, 2003), 1–9.

16. Smith, "Religion, Social Conflict," 7.

17. Phan, *Christianities in Asia*, 5. A very interesting study was made by Jonathan Fox on how religion contributes to violent conflicts and also to nonviolent protests. He insightfully observes that violence more readily crosses religious lines than do peaceful protests. See Jonathan Fox, "Is Ethnoreligious Conflict a Contagious Disease?," *Studies in Conflict and Terrorism* 27 (2004): 89–106.

18. Song, *Theology from the Womb of Asia*, 38–40. From 1945 to 1949, nations that were formerly under colonial rule, such as Indonesia, Korea, Philippines, India, and Burma, won their independence, with China establishing a communist regime after

will see how Christians in Korea and China appropriated the doctrine of eschatology in their specific contexts.

A Tale of Two Koreas

1. Eschatology and the "Queen of Suffering"

In protesting the persecution of Christians to Roman authorities, Tertullian wrote in his *Apologeticus*, "The oftener we are mown down by you, the more in number we grow; *the blood of* Christians *is seed*." More than a century later this statement would again be proven true by Christians in Korea. Because of the great suffering they have endured in history, Ham Sok Hon, the "Korean Gandhi," called Korea the "Queen of Suffering," and described his nation's suffering in this vivid manner: "Haven't you all nailed my mother to a cross and exposed her private parts to her shame, Red China holding her one arm and Japan grasping the other, while the polar bear holds down her head and the eagle from Rocky Mountains holds down her legs?"[19] Two interlinked events in the history of the Korean Presbyterian Church demonstrate how the Koreans suffered: first, in relation to the early spread of Protestantism, and second, concerning the issue of the Shinto Shrines. In these, eschatology played a vital role in upholding and nourishing the growth of the church.

The Korean church grew rapidly between 1895 and 1907. This was a time of great sociopolitical upheaval as the nation was the focal point of two wars that Imperial Japan won: against the Qing Empire in the First Sino-Japanese War (1894–1895) and against the Russian Empire in the Russo-Japanese War (1904–1905). With the Japanese colonization of Korea in 1910, Korean Christians experienced continuous persecution,

---

several years under civil war. Imperial Japan, of course, was dismantled and became a democratic nation. However, independence was not absolute in some cases, as exemplified in Korea. While 1945 brought an end to Japanese colonial rule, it also marked the beginning of Korea's division into North and South and falling under the influence of the Soviet Union and the United States, respectively.

19. This is also the title of his work. See Ham Sok Hon, *Queen of Suffering: A Spiritual History of Korea*, trans. E. Sang Yu, ed. John Sullivan (London: Friends World Committee for Consultation, 1985), x; quoted in Peter Koslowski, ed., *The Origin and the Overcoming of Evil and Suffering in the World Religions* (Dordrecht: Springer, 2001), 9.

first because of their nationality and later also because of their faith.[20] The failure of the 1919 nonviolent protest against Japan by the Samil Independence Movement, which was led by many Korean Christians, became a crucial turning point as the Japanese retaliated ruthlessly by placing thousands in prison and murdering many Korean believers.[21]

This led the people to despair about their sociopolitical situation, and contributed to the appeal of premillennial eschatology. During this period of colonization, some notable Korean Presbyterians led by Sun Joo Kil, also called the "Father of Korean Christianity," Ik Doo Kim, and Hyung Yong Park persuasively taught and preached a future-oriented and other-worldly Christianity. Ik Doo Kim's emphasis, for instance, "on the millennial Kingdom and eschatology harmonized well with the hope of a suffering people who lost independence and sovereignty during the annexation."[22] The churches thus fixed their eyes on a future world, for the present world was incapable of being saved, and, that being so, Christian duty was perceived in personal and individualistic terms: to preach deliverance, to witness, baptize, and gather out God's elect in preparation for Christ's second coming.[23]

Premillennialism reached the Korean church through Western missionaries who were deeply influenced by D. L. Moody and Arthur Pierson, two pioneers of the eschatological missionary movement after the American Civil War.[24] Through their leadership, the movement spread among college and seminary students. Pierson's concept of "evangelization of the world in this generation" inspired a flood of

20. Ung Kyu Pak, *Millennialism in the Korean Protestant Church* (New York: Peter Lang, 2005), 109. A good overview of the history of Roman Catholic and Protestant Christianity in Korea can be found in Ig-Jin Kim's *History and Theology of Korean Pentecostalism: Sunbogeum (Pure Gospel) Pentecostalism* (Zoetermeer, Netherlands: Uitgeverij Boeckencentrum, 2003), 31–52.

21. Doug Sung Choi, "The Roots of Presbyterian Conflicts in Korea, 1910–1954, and the Predominance of Orthodoxy" (PhD diss., Emory University, 1992), 143–144.

22. Kwang Jin Paik, "Korean Presbyterianism and the Kingdom Expectation: The Role of Eschatological Motive in the Expansion of the Korean Presbyterian Church, 1884–1945" (PhD diss., Reformed Theological Seminary, 1996), 155; quoting Yong Kyu Park, "Korean Presbyterianism and Biblical Authority: The Role of Scripture in the Shaping of Korean Presbyterianism, 1918–1953," PhD diss. (Trinity Evangelical Divinity School, 1991), 239.

23. Paul Hang-Sik Cho, *Eschatology and Ecology: Experiences of the Korean Church* (Oxford: Regnum, 2010), 153.

24. Jaekeun Lee, "McCormick Missionaries and the Shaping of Korean Evangelical Presbyterianism," MTh diss. (University of Edinburgh, 2010), 38.

volunteers who understood Christ's return to be imminent, so his fol-
lowers needed to spread the gospel all over the world.[25]

Korea proved to be fertile ground. Timothy S. Lee incisively points
out that when Protestant missionaries reached Korea, the people were
also searching for a new moral order that the existing ones such as
Buddhism, Confucianism, and the *Sirhak* (Practical Learning) movement
of the Choson dynasty had failed to adequately provide.[26] Unhappily,
the Puritanical attitude of many early missionaries and their dualistic
view toward the world and society inculcated among many Korean
Christians a faith that was hostile to indigenous religion and culture.[27]
Nonetheless, this did not lead to a total rejection of traditional or folk
beliefs. Hang-Sik Cho argues that Christianity in Korea incorporated
many aspects of shamanism, which came about through a "cultural
colorization" of Christian experience and the spontaneous syncretiza-
tion by Koreans with shamanistic backgrounds.[28] In other words, "the
beliefs of Shamanism have enabled Koreans to comprehend more easily
the references in Christianity to the idea of God, to evil in the world,
to heaven and hell, and to benevolent and evil spirits."[29] This, as we
will see shortly, is a charge that has been levelled against David Yonggi
Cho, leader of one of the largest churches in the world, the Yoido Full
Gospel Church.

The new Christian faith that the Koreans embraced was put to the
test by the "Shinto Shrine" issue. After conquering Manchuria, the Japanese government coerced the Korean people to worship at the Shinto
shrine, which included performance of religious rites. For the Korean
Presbyterian Church, the issue was not merely about a political act of
loyalty to the state, or a matter of nonessentials; it was about the very

25. Paik, "Korean Presbyterianism," 77–79.

26. Timothy S. Lee, *Born Again: Evangelicalism in Korea* (Honolulu: University of
Hawaii, 2010), 3–7.

27. Keel Hee-Sung, "Can Korean Protestantism Be Reconciled with Culture? Rethinking Theology and Culture in Korea," *Inter-Religio* 24 (Winter 1993): 50.

28. Hang-Sik Cho, *Eschatology and Ecology*. A good study of shamanism in Korea was
carried out by Tongshik Ryu in "Shamanism: the Dominant Folk Religion in Korea,"
Inter-Religio 5 (Spring 1984): 8–15.

29. Boo Woon Yoo, "Response to Shamanism by the Pentecostal Church," *International Review of Mission* 75 (Jan. 1986): 72–73. Yoo adds that "the above characteristics,
developed through belief in shamanism, greatly affected the Korean appropriation
and expression of Christianity, through revival and Pentecostal enthusiasm and an
other-worldly orientation."

core of the Christian faith, for it entailed a religious act of worshipping other gods.[30] The Korean Presbyterian Church resisted, which led to the imprisonment of more than 5,000 Christians and the shuttering of around 1,200 Presbyterian churches.

An important factor enabling the Presbyterian Church to endure Japanese persecution and resist the oppressive measure was its premillennial outlook. Prominent leaders of the Anti-Shinto or Non-Shrine Worship Movement, such as Ki-Sun Lee and Ki-Cheul Ju, were convinced of Christ's impending coming that would bring about the fall of all political nations and the establishment of the millennial kingdom. Hence, they exhorted Korean believers to take courage in opposing the Japanese Empire. As the martyred Ju said, the Korean church must dare to die for Jesus, for others, and for the defense of the Christian faith.[31]

2. Eschatological Blessings: Yonggi Cho and the Yoido Full Gospel Church

The Korean people experienced untold suffering yet again when the nation was devastated by the Korean War. It would have been easy to lose hope in this situation. But believing in the gospel message and in the power of the Holy Spirit to give hope to the hopeless, David Yonggi Cho pioneered a "tent church" just a few years after the war in the slums of Dae-jo dong. It was a foundational experience for Cho, who experienced deeply what it meant to be one with his people in that time of utter despair.[32] Hence, his primary motivation for preaching in those early days was to give a message of hope. Cho recounts: "I started preaching to people in the cursed land of Korea after the war. It was war-torn, broken, destroyed, and poverty-stricken. I had nothing materially to give to the people, but I was putting spiritual resources into their mind . . . Spiritual resources are the most powerful kind of resource. Without them you cannot have material victory . . . Soon they got out

---

30. Harvie M. Conn, "Studies in the Theology of the Korean Presbyterian Church," *Westminster Theological Journal* 29, no. 2 (May 1967): 165–166; Kim, *History and Theology of Korean Pentecostalism*, 74–75.

31. Pak, *Millennialism in the Korean Protestant Church*, 191–192; Paik, "Korean Presbyterianism," 193.

32. David Yonggi Cho, *Salvation, Health and Prosperity: Our Threefold Blessings in Christ* (Altamonte Springs: Creation House, 1987), 11.

of their poverty-stricken situation. Jesus Christ through His crucifixion successfully destroyed the curse."[33]

By 1961, Yoido Full Gospel Central Church had grown to 300 members; 100,000 in 1979; 250,000 in 1983; over half a million in 1987. By 2006, it was listed as having 700,000 members.[34] Certainly, much credit can be attributed to Cho for his multiple skills, but, as Wonsuk Ma points out, the bedrock of his ministry that has fueled the phenomenal growth of Yoido Church is his "theology of blessing."[35] This refers to Cho's teaching on the Fivefold Gospel and Threefold Blessing. The former refers to Jesus's role as Savior, Healer, Blesser, Baptizer, and Coming King; while the latter, also called "treble blessings," is based on 3 John 2 which refers to the salvation of the soul, health and healing of the body, and material wealth from God.[36]

The fifth element of the Fivefold Gospel, Jesus as Coming King or the Gospel of the Second Coming, refers to Cho's dispensational premillennialism perspective on eschatology. His view conforms to the classic Pentecostal perspective, but, as Ig-Jin Kim remarks, the real strength of Cho's eschatology is its application in daily life.[37] This is based on Cho's already-but-not-yet view of God's kingdom. Whereas the earlier Korean Presbyterian Church emphasized the future advent of Christ and the establishment of the millennium, for Cho, the "here" and "now" are also important. Healing, miracles, and the third aspect of the treble

33. David Yonggi Cho, *My Church Growth Stories* (Seoul: Seoul Logos Co., 2006), 157.

34. Vincent Leoh, "Eschatology and Pneumatic Preaching with a Case of David Yonggi Cho," *Asian Journal of Pentecostal Studies* 10, no. 1 (2007): 111.

35. Wonsuk Ma, "David Yonggi Cho's Theology of Blessing: Basis, Legitimacy, and Limitations," *Evangelical Review of Theology* 35, no. 2 (2011): 143. Cho, of course, has been criticized from various quarters. Gordon Fee, the General Presbytery of the Assemblies of God, US evangelicals, Robert Schuller, and others have refuted Cho's teachings. See Allan Anderson, "The Contribution of David Yonggi Cho to a Contextual Theology in Korea," *Journal of Pentecostal Theology* 12, no. 1 (2003): 89–90.

36. Ma, "Cho's Theology of Blessing," 144. Ma makes the good point that the theological language of Cho's five-fold theology is closely aligned with the "Pentecostal Four" of the Assemblies of God, to which Cho is known to be affiliated. See also Kim, *History and Theology of Korean Pentecostalism*, 202–206. As to the origin of Cho's teaching on the treble blessings, Myung Soo Park maintains that Cho derived it from Oral Roberts. Myung Soo Park, "David Yonggi Cho and International Pentecostal/Charismatic Movements," *Journal of Pentecostal Theology* 12, no. 1 (2003): 108.

37. Kim, *History and Theology of Korean Pentecostalism*, 304. See also Hwa Yung, "The Missional Challenge of David Yonggi Cho's Theology," *Asian Journal of Pentecostal Studies* 7, no. 1 (2004): 71–73.

blessings, material wealth, are therefore important manifestations of the presence of the in-breaking kingdom.

Because of Cho's emphasis on material blessings as an aspect of eschatology that others see as excessive, his theology is branded as *Gibok Shinang* (faith that seeks or prays for blessing).[38] As Cho says, "If we do not receive the 'riches' as stated in scripture, we make the poverty of Jesus of no effect. We have an important responsibility: to receive the prosperous life . . . which He makes possible for us by living in poverty."[39]

This emphasis on material blessings has led many from both within and without to identify it as a local brand of America's "prosperity gospel," and as a shamanization of Christianity in Korea. Harvey Cox is known to have claimed that, as exemplified by Yoido Church, a crucial reason "for Korean Pentecostalism's extraordinary growth is its unerring ability to absorb huge chunks of indigenous Korean shamanism and demon possession into its worship."[40] However, those who disagree with such assessments point to, among other key factors, the uniqueness of the Korean context. As Hwa Yung suggests, "a proper understanding of Cho on this is to see it as illustrative of his efforts to contextualize the gospel in order to address the felt needs of a people."[41] In his insightful study, Chuong Kwon Cho connects the Korean notion of *Han* as a "contextual factor" that Cho and Yoido, as "institutional factors," are able to address adequately.[42]

38. Ma, "Cho's Theology of Blessing," 147.

39. Yonggi Cho, *Salvation, Health and Prosperity*, 68.

40. Harvey Cox, *Fire from Heaven: The Rise of Pentecostal Spirituality and the Reshaping of Religion in the Twenty-First Century* (London: Cassell, Petter, Galpin & Co., 1996), 222. A good overview of criticisms of Cho on this aspect is given by Allan Anderson in "Contribution of David Yonggi Cho," 89–93.

41. Hwa Yung, "The Missiological Challenge of David Yonggi Cho's Theology," *Asian Journal of Pentecostal Studies* 7, no. 1 (2004): 75–76. See also Ma, "Cho's Theology of Blessing," 145–148; Anderson, "Contribution of David Yonggi Cho," 93–99. Park also asserts that instead of drawing from Korean shamanism, Cho drew from the American Pentecostal/charismatic movements in regard to his teachings on material wealth. Park, "Cho and International Pentecostal/Charismatic Movements," 127.

42. Chuong Kwon Cho, "*Han* and the Pentecostal Experience: A Study of the Growth of the Yoido Full Gospel Church in Korea," PhD diss. (University of Birmingham, 2010), 48. Chuong points to three aspects of *Han*: (1) Korean despair; (2) the oppressed minds of the Korean Minjung; and (3) the Korean cultural archetype.

China

1. China's End-Time Calling: The Back to Jerusalem Movement

Eschatology has often played a vital role in Christian missions, especially in relation to the Great Commission. For Christians in China's house churches it is the central motivation. As one of the leaders of the house churches says, "We believe God has given us a solemn responsibility to take the fire from his altar and complete the Great Commission by establishing his kingdom in all of the remaining countries and people groups in Asia, the Middle East, and Islamic North Africa. When this happens, we believe that the Scripture says the Lord Jesus will return for his bride."[43]

Napoleon's assessment of China – "There is a sleeping giant. Let her sleep. For when she wakes, she will shake the world" – can be aptly related to the massive growth of Christianity in that nation.[44] Chinese Christians in the last century have certainly awakened, and a particular house church network, the Back to Jerusalem Movement (BJM), has shaken the Christian world with its vision to bring back the gospel to its roots by preaching and establishing fellowships in all the countries, cities, and towns among all ethnic groups between China and Jerusalem.[45]

While many believe that missionary efforts are rooted in Western imperialism, the Back to Jerusalem Movement (BJM) is an indigenous movement that defies such analysis.[46] The movement, says Timothy Tennent, is not under a single organization, but "is more of a vision statement that many Chinese Christians have identified with, and yet which provides no formal connection among its adherents."[47] The BJM emerged in Shandong Province in the 1920s from independent Chinese churches. Originally part of the Jesus Family house church network,

43. Quoted in Paul Hattaway, *Back to Jerusalem: Three Chinese House Church Leaders Share Their Vision to Complete the Great Commission* (Carlisle: Piquant, 2003), 20.

44. James Sung-Hwan Park, "Chosen to Fulfill the Great Commission? Biblical and Theological Reflections on the Back to Jerusalem Vision of Chinese Churches," *Missiology: An International Review* 43, no. 2 (2015): 163–164.

45. Hattaway, *Back to Jerusalem*, x.

46. Tim Stafford, "A Captivating Vision: Why Chinese House Churches May Just End Up Fulfilling the Great Commission," *Christianity Today* 48, no. 4 (April 2004): 1.

47. Timothy C. Tennent, *Theology in the Context of World Christianity: How the Global Church Is Influencing the Way We Think about and Discuss Theology* (Grand Rapids: Zondervan, 2007), 238.

some members later formed the Northwest Spiritual Movement that Simon Zhao led in the 1940s. Their vision was to preach the gospel in Xinjiang and beyond. Another Chinese leader, Mark Ma from Shaanxi Province, confirmed Zhao's vision with a vision he also received, which entailed taking the gospel outside China, through Islamic countries, and all the way back to Jerusalem.[48] The missionary Helen Bailey would call this group the "Back to Jerusalem Evangelistic Band."[49] Currently the movement envisions having by the year 2030 some 20,000 Chinese missionaries who will join the global missions force.[50]

Premillennial eschatology adapted to the Chinese situation figures prominently in the BJM. It holds that Chinese Christians have been specially called by God to help usher in the second coming of Christ by fulfilling the Great Commission (Matt 24:14). Tobias Brandner observes that BJM's eschatological vision has functional psychological implications for Chinese Christians, who have been asking why Christianity has grown very late in China and what role God has for them in the history of salvation.[51] To such questions the BJM gives a narrative of history that depicts a shift toward China in God's covenantal relationship, especially now that America has lost its calling due to its history of political aggression. Other cities and nations in the past have also been called by God for a special purpose, like Israel, Wittenberg, Zurich, Geneva, and, more recently, America.[52] But in these end times, with their history of persecution, Chinese Christians are perfectly situated to enter into this unique covenant with God.

It must be recalled that Christians in China experienced persecution at the hands of the communist regime from 1950 when the Communist Party supported the formation of the Three-Self Patriotic Movement (TSPM), which aimed to unify all Chinese Protestant churches under the Communist Party's leadership. Of those persecuted, the indigenous

---

48. [Name witheld], "Assisting House Churches to Become Great Commission Churches" (PhD diss., Southern Baptist Theological Seminary, 2012), 157–158; Hattaway, *Back to Jerusalem*, 12.

49. Park, "Chosen to Fulfill the Great Commission?," 165.

50. Steve Z., "Indigenous Mission Movements in China," *Mission Roundtable: The OMF Journal for Reflective Practitioners* 11, no. 3 (Sept–Dec 2016), 27.

51. Tobias Brandner, "Trying to Make Sense of History: Chinese Christian Traditions of Countercultural Belief and Their Theological and Political Interpretation of Past and Present History," *Studies in World Christianity* 17, no. 3 (2011): 219.

52. Brandner, "Trying to Make Sense of History," 220.

Protestant movements suffered the most.[53] Thus, Liu Zhenying, more famously known as "Brother Yun" and a key leader of the BJM, said, "there is little that any of the Muslim, Buddhist, or Hindu countries can do to us that we haven't already experienced in China."[54] Their crucial role in these end times thus gives Chinese Christians much assurance as they seek to provide the people with an alternative interpretation of their nation's history, especially amid the nation's current experience of economic success, which the BJM also sees as bringing decay to the nation's traditional values.[55]

From an eschatological standpoint, therefore, the BJM understands God to have orchestrated cultural, political, and socioeconomic factors to prepare them for their special calling. Their ability to speak different languages, knowledge of various cultures, good relationship with Arabs, ability to enter Arab nations without much suspicion, and aptitude for holding meetings in house churches make them appropriate messengers of the gospel.[56] And as Christians in the Middle East are experiencing severe persecution from violent extremists, Christina Lin writes encouragingly: "As darkness descends upon the region, a light is kindling in the East and spreading west on the Silk Road towards this heart of darkness. What is not reported in mainstream media is that Christianity in the Mideast is not yet facing extinction, as new Christians from the East are migrating to help in the region – Chinese Christians. China, currently experiencing the largest Christian movement in the world, is marching west."[57]

---

53. Yihua Xu, "'Patriotic' Protestants: The Making of an Official Church," in *God and Caesar in China: Policy Implications of Church–State Tensions*, ed. Jason Kindopp and Carol Lee Hamrin (Washington DC: Brookings Institution, 2004), 115, 118. The "three selves" stand for self-governing, self-support, and self-propagation. These principles were meant to assure the government that the member Protestant churches were free from foreign influence and supportive of the new communist regime. Rodney Star and Xiuhua Wang, *A Star in the East: The Rise of Christianity in China* (West Conshohocken: Templeton, 2015), 44–45.

54. Quoted in Hattaway, *Back to Jerusalem*, 58.

55. Tobias Bandner, "Premillennial and Countercultural Faith and Its Production and Reception in the Chinese Context," *Asian Journal of Pentecostal Studies* 14, no. 1 (2011): 8–9.

56. J. Park, "Chosen to Fulfill the Great Commission?," 165–168.

57. Christina Lin, "China's Back to Jerusalem Movement," *ISPSW Strategy Series* 329 (March 2015): 2.

2. Watchman Nee

Among Chinese Christian leaders, Watchman Nee (Ni Tuosheng) has the distinction of having immense influence both in China and in the global Christian world. He converted to Christianity as a young man during the 1920s, and by the time the Communists came to power in Mainland China in 1949, the indigenous church movement he founded, "the Little Flock," already had 70,000 members.[58] As China was undergoing social and political upheaval during the first half of the twentieth century, Christian leaders such as Nee inevitably addressed the social situation that confronted Chinese Christians. His perspective on eschatology played a vital role in this matter.[59]

Through the missionary Margaret E. Barber, Nee came to embrace Brethren ideas such as the absence of church government beyond the local congregation and the dispensational, premillennialist eschatology of the influential Brethren teacher J. N. Darby.[60] Using the New Testament church as a model, Nee rejected denominationalism and the then-prevailing Western "missionary culture" that presupposed foreign superiority over local Chinese leaders, who were merely hired as "native assistants" of foreign mission agencies instead of getting called by congregations.[61] When the Three-Self Patriotic Movement (TSPM) was established in 1950 calling for indigenization and ecclesial autonomy, Nee believed that the Little Flock embodied those ideals and hence would be tolerated by the communist state. The party state and the TSPM, however, also intended to control churches for the Maoist state, and thus continued to view Nee and the Little Flock church as a

---

58. Archie Hui, "The Pneumatology of Watchman Nee: A New Testament Perspective," *The Evangelical Quarterly* 75, no. 4 (2003): 3; Liu Yi, "Globalization of Chinese Christianity: A Study of Watchman Nee and Witness Lee's Ministry," *Asia Journal of Theology* 30, no. 1 (April 2016): 98.

59. Kevin Xiyi Yao, "Chinese Evangelicals and Social Concerns: A Historical and Comparative Overview," in *After Imperialism: Christian Identity in China and the Global Evangelical Movement*, ed. Richard R. Cook and David W. Pao (Cambridge: Lutterworth, 2012): 52–53.

60. Joseph Tse-Hei Lee, "Watchman Nee and the Little Flock Movement in Maoist China," *Church History* 74, no. 1 (March 2005): 73–74.

61. Alexander Chow, *Theosis, Sino-Christian Theology and the Second Chinese Enlightenment: Heaven and Humanity in Unity* (New York: Palgrave Macmillan, 2013), 55–56; Grace Y. May, "Watchman Nee and the Breaking of Bread: The Missiological and Spiritual Forces That Contributed to an Indigenous Chinese Ecclesiology" (ThD diss., Boston University School of Theology, 2000), 252–253.

threat. He was arrested in 1952 and in 1956 charged with various crimes against the state. Nee died in prison in 1972.[62]

Following Darby and C. I. Scofield's eschatology, Nee developed a dualistic and pessimistic perspective of society and human history. The turbulence in China only confirmed his convictions.[63] The world, said Nee, is organized by Satan into a system that is antithetical to God. While acknowledging that the world evinces a certain movement toward progress, the crucial question for Nee was: "To what is this 'progress' tending?" The systems that give the world its appearance of coherence – politics, education, art, commerce, law, music – all move toward the setting up in history of the kingdom of the antichrist.[64] He said "that there is absolutely no solution to the problems of the present system, governments, and society. The problems will be taken care of. When the new heaven and the new earth are inaugurated, the old order with all of its problems will be borne away. Today we do not take care of those problems. We only save people. Even though society at large will be somewhat affected after individuals are saved, our commission is not to save the world."[65]

Nee emphasized that "Jesus never touched the question of politics. . . . He came to save individuals from sins. . . . His purpose is to save man. He has no intention other than this."[66] Bernard Erling is thus correct in his assertion that "there is no suggestion anywhere in Nee's writings that a part of the Christian's responsibility is to seek to build a better world. . . . The world may be used to advance the evangelistic

---

62. Tse-Hei Lee, "Watchman Nee," 82–87; Bernard Erling, "The Story of Watchman Nee," *The Lutheran Quarterly* 28, no. 2 (May 1976): 146–147. A good account of the trial is in chapter 18 of Nee's biography by Angus I. Kinnear, *Against the Tide: The Story of Watchman Nee* (Fort Washington: Christian Literature Crusade, 1974).

63. Nee's most profound influences are from the Pietist background of the Brethren founders J. N. Darby and George Müller. The writings of dispensationalists, particularly G. H. Pember, Robert Govett, and D. M. Panton, influenced Nee's eschatology. Ken Ang Lee, "Watchman Nee: A Study of His Major Theological Themes," PhD diss. (Westminster Theological Seminary, 1989), 49–53.

64. Watchman Nee, *Love Not the World*, ed. Angus I. Kinnear (Fort Washington: Christian Literature Crusade, 1970), 12, 14.

65. Watchman Nee, *The Normal Christian Faith* (Anaheim: Living Stream Ministry, 1993), 178.

66. Nee, *Normal Christian Faith*, 178–179.

efforts of the church, but Nee is wholly pessimistic with respect to programs of social reform."[67]

For Nee and other Chinese evangelicals of his time, such as Wang Ming-dao, sin is the ultimate cause of the world's depraved condition, and no amount of participation in the social-political sphere will be able to put the world back to its proper purpose. In line with dispensational premillennialism, Nee urgently called his listeners to a life of personal holiness and evangelism.[68] It is not that Nee was against social action altogether. Rather, as Ken Ang Lee points out, the threat Nee and other evangelical leaders "perceived in the Social Gospel was not its emphasis on social concern per se. It was that it emphasized social concern in an exclusivistic way which seemed to undercut the relevance of the message of the Gospel itself."[69]

While Nee looked to Christ's second coming to usher in God's kingdom, he did not consider the world to be in utter chaos. It is indeed fallen, but God has set up earthly governments, and to them Christians owe *limited* submission. As Nee pointed out emphatically, "God alone is the object of our absolute obedience."[70]

Cruciform Eschatology

The foregoing accounts illustrate how Christians in Korea and China confronted the social and political realities of their time armed with the Christian eschatological vision that was articulated through premillennial eschatology. The responses they gave to those particular realities certainly also sought to answer the question that, while in prison, Dietrich Bonhoeffer asked: "Who is Christ for us today?"[71]

The christological emphasis of the question is central to eschatology, and indeed to the Christian view of history. Jesus Christ, according to Yeo Khiok-Khng, "defines the end (purpose, goal and fulfillment) of history.... Jesus infuses history with meaning, redeeming and consum-

---

67. Erling, "Story of Watchman Nee," 154.

68. Chow, *Theosis*, 59.

69. Ang Lee, "Watchman Nee," 231.

70. Watchman Nee, *Take Heed* (New York: Christian Fellowship Publishers, 1991), 47–50.

71. Dietrich Bonhoeffer, *Letters and Papers from Prison*, ed. Eberhard Bethge (New York: Collier, 1972), 279.

mating history."[72] Pointing out further the significance of the crucified Christ in the future restoration of all things that takes into account the transitory restoration of the oppressed in history, Moltmann remarks, "with the raising of the crucified Christ from the dead, the future of the new creation of all things has already begun in the midst of this dying and transitory world."[73]

Christian eschatology, as mentioned at the beginning of this essay, can only be understood in the context of God's reign that the Christ-event inaugurated. Paul Löffler said it well: "The beginning of the reign of God as an event of history . . . and as a hope to be fully realized in the future is the context of the life and ministry of Jesus as well as the key to his words and deeds."[74] This entails perceiving Jesus's earthly ministry to the poor and his confrontations with oppressive powers that led ultimately to the cross as the very shape of God's advancing eschatological kingdom. In other words, God's eschatological kingdom is cruciform. Again, Löffler is instructive when he says that "the suffering of Christ, understood in the context of the beginning kingdom of God, raises above all the issue of power, of the counterpower of Christ versus the established powers of this world."[75]

As an eschatological community, the church therefore needs to go beyond exclaiming "Conversion alone!" by proclaiming the gospel exclusively to the inner recesses of the human heart so that individu-

---

72. K. K. Yeo, "An Eschatological View of History in the New Testament: Messianic and Millennarian Hope," *Asian Journal of Theology* 15, no. 1 (April 2001): 43. See also his *Chairman Mao Meets the Apostle Paul: Christianity, Communism, and the Hope of China* (Grand Rapids: Brazos, 2002), 27–56; *Musing with Confucius and Paul: Toward a Chinese Christian Theology* (Eugene: Cascade, 2008), 126–131; and *What Has Jerusalem to Do with Beijing? Biblical Interpretation from a Chinese Perspective* (Eugene: Pickwick, 2018), 194–241.

73. Jürgen Moltmann, *The Coming of God: Christian Eschatology* (London: SCM, 1996), 136; Brandon Lee Morgan, "Eschatology for the Oppressed: Millenarianism and Liberation in the Eschatology of Jürgen Moltmann," *Perspectives in Religious Studies* 39, no. 4 (Winter 2012): 379, 381. In *The Coming of God*, Moltmann's christological basis for his eschatology is found on 194–196. A more expanded explanation can be found in his work *The Way of Jesus Christ: Christology in Messianic Dimensions* (Minneapolis: Fortress, 1993), 181–196.

74. Paul Löffler, "The Reign of God Has Come in the Suffering Christ: An Exploration of the Power of the Powerless," *International Review of Mission* 68, no. 270 (April 1979): 110. See also Yeo, "Eschatological View of History," 39.

75. Löffler, "Reign of God," 111.

als will be taken to heaven away from the earth.[76] It must be ready to follow Jesus, even to the point of suffering, in disclosing concretely and witnessing to God's character of love, justice, and righteousness in anticipation of the fulfillment of his future reign. Kosuke Koyama is right in saying that because God's nature is to be involved with others in history, the "eschatology of the Bible has this basic orientation toward the others."[77]

This World or the Other?

Yonggi Cho's this-worldly eschatology had its contextual roots in Korea's wartime sufferings. Although trained under classical Pentecostal missionaries, his experiences with the suffering Korean people, coupled with a shift in Pentecostal attention to a this-worldly eschatology in the 1960s, helped shape his theology of blessing.[78] Shirley Ho points to similar contextual factors in the case of Taiwanese Christians who have embraced what she calls "Taiwan Philo-Semitic Theology" (TPST), or a theological preoccupation with Jews/Israel. According to Ho, Taiwan's "underdog" experience and shamanistic culture contributed to their seeking material blessings, as well as their finding a closer affinity with the Jews who are known for their wealth.[79]

Cho's theology of wealth certainly has some contextual and biblical-theological basis[80] and it provides answers to the material longings of

76. Roko Kerovec, "The Resurrection of Christ and the Eschatological Vision of the Kingdom of God as the Platform for Evangelistic Practice: The Challenges and Possibilities of the Evangelistic Commission," *Kairos: Evangelical Journal of Theology* 2, no. 2 (2008): 191–192.

77. Kosuke Koyama, "The Asian Approach to Christ," *Missiology: An International Review* 12, no. 4 (Oct. 1984): 440. See Denis Edwards, *How God Acts: Creation, Redemption, and Special Divine Action* (Minneapolis: Fortress, 2010), 26–33.

78. Wonsuk Ma, "Pentecostal Eschatology: What Happened When the Wave Hit the West End of the Ocean," *Asian Journal of Pentecostal Studies* 12, no. 1 (2009): 103.

79. Shirley S. Ho, "The Philosemitic Theology on the Eschatological Restoration of Israel in Taiwan Christianity," (paper presented at the Annual American Academy of Religion and Society of Biblical Literature, Boston, MA, Nov. 2017), 15–16. Like TPST, the early Pentecostals embraced philosemitism mainly upon their appropriation of dispensational premillennialism. See Eric Nelson Newberg, *The Pentecostal Mission: The Legacy of Pentecostal Zionism* (Eugene: Pickwick, 2012), 209–213.

80. See Ma, "Cho's Theology of Blessing," 145–158; Yung, "Missiological Challenge," 70–76.

many of Asia's poor. It is nonetheless also fraught with peril. Korea's Tonghap Presbyterian denomination released a study of Cho's theology of blessing in 1983 and stated, among other things, that it tended toward teaching spiritual salvation as a means of receiving blessings in this earthly life, thus connecting God's salvation with worldliness and success-centeredness.[81] Ma also points out that the theology of blessing is "by nature self-centered," and if it fails to integrate what authentic Christian discipleship means, then its adherents may simply measure the quality of their lives by the blessings they have; ask God for wealth merely out of selfish interests; and seek blessings through unjust and oppressive means. The theological purpose of the blessings is thus of crucial importance.[82]

In contrast, the early Korean Presbyterian Church, Watchman Nee, and the Back to Jerusalem Movement (BJM) took a mainly other-worldly orientation. The early Pentecostals also looked to Christ's imminent return and similarly became preoccupied with missionary zeal for winning souls. Like the BJM and the Korean Presbyterians, Pentecostal missionaries from the West, including Filipino *balikbayans* (returning overseas residents) in the 1940s, were convinced, especially after experiencing Spirit baptism, that the Christian calling is primarily about proclaiming the gospel.[83]

Without denigrating the biblical mandate concerning the missionary enterprise, as well as the sufferings that Nee and the other Christians in Asia have experienced, the consequences of their other-worldly eschatology must not be overlooked. One key concern is related to Christian social responsibility. With a particular focus on the imminent return of Christ and the future realization of God's kingdom, Nee and the others were pessimistic about the affairs of this world so they disregarded the eschatological import of the church's responsibility to society. Korea's Hang-Sik Cho puts it this way: "the most devastating eschatological teaching in respect to structural social change is a pessimistic fatalism concerning social conditions . . . as espoused by dispensational premillennialists."[84] Here we see the acute relationship between eschatology and ethics. As Rian Venter says incisively, "eschatology is

---

81. Kim, *Korean Pentecostalism*, 207.

82. Ma, "Cho's Theology of Blessing," 158. See also Juliet Ma, "Eschatology and Mission: Living the 'Last Days' Today," *Transformation* 26, no. 3 (July 2009): 195–196.

83. Ma, "Pentecostal Eschatology," 99.

84. Hang-Sik Cho, *Eschatology and Ecology*, 192.

fundamentally an ethical project – it has performative effects."[85] Or, in this instance, non-performative.

Justice in the here and now is thus a casualty of such an other-worldly eschatology. Social reforms, engagement in the public sphere, and care for nature and the environment are generally deemed unimportant, since the world is a sinking ship.[86] This notion actually expresses a dualistic cosmology in which the old heaven and earth are expected to pass away to give way to the new (e.g., 2 Pet 3:7) that are not located in the same historical continuity.[87] But if the eschatological kingdom of God is intertwined with the historical Christ-event – his life, death, and resurrection – then not only do the old and the new heaven and earth share the same historical platform, but the kingdom of God must also be seen in the context of time and space.[88] Justice, similarly, must be in time and space. That is, it must be historically, culturally, and socially located. As Bradley A. Johnson notes, based on the apostle Paul's unveiling of a new creation in line with Romans 2:13–14, justice must be achievable in the present. It is not something that only an apocalypse can bring. "Justice, in short, need not be an appeal to, or a promise of, a change in reality that comes from beyond existing reality. If we are to do justice to justice, we will allow it to become possible – to become transformative now."[89]

Conclusion: Cruciform Eschatology in Asia

"The time is fulfilled, and the kingdom of God has come near; repent, and believe in the gospel" (Mark 1:15). To the multitudes of Asia's poor

85. Rian Venter, "Trends in Contemporary Christian Eschatological Reflection," *Missionalia* 43, no. 1 (2015): 115.

86. Adherents of premillennialism are of course not homogeneous in their doctrine and practice, like the revivalists of the late nineteenth century who held on to a pessimistic outlook on the world but, in contrast with other premillennialists of their time, persisted in their social relief work to prepare the poor in receiving the gospel. Bernie A. Van De Walle, *The Heart of the Gospel: A. B. Simpson, the Fourfold Gospel, and Late Nineteenth-Century Evangelical Theology* (Eugene: Pickwick, 2009), 49–51. In regard to dispensationalism and ecology, see Hang-Sik Cho, *Eschatology and Ecology*, 222–224.

87. Kerovec, "Resurrection of Christ," 193.

88. Kerovec, 192–193.

89. Bradley A. Johnson, "Doing Justice to Justice: Re-Assessing Deconstructive Eschatology," *Political Theology* 12, no. 1 (2011): 22–23.

and oppressed, Jesus's proclamation of the in-breaking of God's eschatological kingdom can only be good news. But, before it can be good
news to them, it must first be so to the churches in Asia, especially in
those nations where Christianity came through colonization. Many
Asians certainly have something in common with the Indians who once
sent this message to Pope John Paul II: "We used to praise our God in
our language, with our gestures and dances, with instruments made
by us, until the day European civilization arrived. It erected the sword,
the language, and the cross, and made us crucified nations."[90] While it
will never be easy for the church in any nation to extricate itself from
its painful past, we do well to remember that it is precisely because of
such experiences that God inaugurated his kingdom through the risen
Christ who was crucified.

In the previous section, the discussion centered on the this-worldly
and other-worldly aspects of eschatology. If we are right in claiming that
God's kingdom has already begun its realization through the Christ-
event, and that it is both a this-worldly and an other-worldly reality,
the question for the church in Asia is not only whether it also embodies
this tension as an eschatological community, but also *from where it comes.*

Koyama insightfully remarks: "Christianity has given humanity a
new concept of center . . . seen in the life and death of Jesus Christ. In
short, Jesus Christ, the center person, establishes his centrality by going
to the periphery . . . by being crucified. . . . Thus, Christianity has made
it possible, through its eschatology, to have a view from the periphery."[91]

Indeed, in poverty-stricken Asia, the church needs to claim the
periphery, where the broken and downtrodden are, as the locus of
God's cruciform eschatological kingdom. Amidst the temptation to
escape from this world by adapting a dehistoricized eschatology or by
rejecting the periphery in light of a this-worldly eschatological gospel
of prosperity, Asian churches are called to be broken themselves and
stretch out their hands in defense of the poor and vulnerable – the
Dalits, the Moros, the Minjung, the Rohingyas, and similarly situated
people. This includes the environment or the earth, which also groans
because of human exploitation (Rom 8:19–25). It is precisely to remind
the church, in Asia and throughout the world, of this important escha-

---

90. K. Koyama, "New World – New Creation: Mission in Power and Faith," *Mission
Studies* 10 (1993): 60 [59–77].

91. Koyama, "Asian Approach to Christ," 445–446.

tological task that Jesus left to us the practice of the Eucharist. David N. Power's reminder aptly concludes this essay:

> Today, at the Lord's table, we need to be particularly mindful of those who have perished through violence, through the senseless death of hunger and illness, or through deprivation of their cultural heritage that is not only a matter of song, dance, and expression, but also of the space and time in which they provide for existence, heritage, and future. To hope even for those dead in the knowledge of the love of God shown in Christ is one of the qualities of eschatological hope, a hope that leads also to action for justice.[92]

For Further Reading

Bergmann, Sigurd, ed. *Eschatology as Imagining the End: Faith between Hope and Despair.* New York: Routledge, 2018.

Braaten, Carl E. *Essays on the Theology and Ethics of the Kingdom of God.* Eugene: Wipf and Stock, 2016.

Phelan Jr., John E. *Essential Eschatology: Our Present and Future Hope.* Downers Grove: IVP Academic, 2013.

Westhelle, Vítor. *Eschatology and Space: The Lost Dimension in Theology Past and Present.* New York: Palgrave Macmillan, 2012.

Wilfred, Felix. *Asian Public Theology: Critical Concerns in Challenging Times.* Delhi: Tercentenary Publication, 2010.

---

92. David N. Power, "Eucharistic Justice," *Theological Studies* 67 (Dec. 2006): 873. In another essay, I relate eucharistic justice to peacemaking initiatives with the Muslims of the Philippines or the *Bangsamoro* people. See Aldrin M. Peñamora, "Eucharistic Justice: A Christ-Centered Response to the Bangsamoro Question in the Philippines," *Asian Journal of Pentecostal Studies* 19, no. 1 (Feb. 2016): 31–44.

CHAPTER 7

From Judeophilia to Ta-Tung in Taiwanese Eschatology

SHIRLEY S. HO

ABSTRACT

After a critical analysis of the prevailing Judeophilia in Taiwanese contemporary churches and eschatological reflections by some Taiwanese Bible commentators, this essay builds on the prophetic text of Isaiah 2:1–5 together with some pertinent New Testament passages and incorporating Chinese political reformer Kang Yu-Wei's vision of *Ta-Tung* to construct a robust Christian eschatology for Taiwan. This is a timely reflection not only for the context in view but also for the global context where nationalism is gaining ground in ecclesiastical and national policies.

Introduction

Over the past few years there has been a resurgence of interest among Chinese Christians in the eschatological restoration of Israel. Interestingly, this renewed interest in Israel's national restoration is evident not only among the Chinese community but also in other cultures.[1] In 2017,

---

1. Don Finto, in *God's Promise and the Future of Israel* (Ventura: Regal, 2006), writes: "Three events are shaping our 21st century: Jewish eyes are opening to the revelation that Yeshua is their Messiah; nations long held in darkness are learning of the God who brings redemption to the world through Israel's famous son; and a centuries-long anti-semitic church is beginning to come alive to the Jewish roots of her faith, to acknowledge her sins and to come together with her Jewish brothers and sisters as one flock in God." (101)

when US President Donald Trump recognized Jerusalem as the capital city of Israel and effected the transfer of the US embassy to Jerusalem, the policy received two opposing reactions around the world: resistance and support. Among Taiwanese Christians, there were apparently those who held a neutral position while others expressed some form of support of the policy, some openly and others clandestinely. However, forceful and outright resistance to the policy was almost absent among Taiwanese Christians. This essay will investigate Taiwanese Christians' views of the eschatological restoration of Israel.

Mindful that the Hebrew Bible contains numerous texts on the subject matter, I have chosen to pay close attention to one: Isaiah 2:1–5. This essay comprises three main sections. I shall first provide a summary of how other Taiwanese Bible commentators read the passage. I shall then highlight a Jewish-centered reading and will discuss the rationale for the adoption of that vision of eschatology. Lastly, guided by Isaiah 2:1–5, New Testament passages, and the reframing of Kang Yu-Wei's *Ta-Tung* utopian conception, I will propose a Taiwanese Christian eschatology which is to be preferred over a Jewish-centered eschatology since it corresponds more faithfully to the biblical witness.

Three representative Chinese readings of Isaiah 2:1–5

Isaiah 2:1–5 is one of the primary texts in Old Testament Zion theology. This short yet promising passage includes numerous important utopian themes: the house of the Lord symbolic of the presence of God in Zion (v. 2); the congregation of an international community of both Jews and gentiles (v. 3a); and adherence to the Torah of the Lord from Zion (v. 3b). It envisages the Lord as the judge over the international community to achieve common goals of peace and harmony by military disarmament (v. 4a). Preoccupation with war and violence will be replaced by agricultural cultivation and development (v. 4b). Finally, "light" will characterize the life of the international community (v. 5).

Zion as Localized Church

The first representative reading of Isaiah 2:1–5 is that of Lin Yong-Tsi, who reads it as a textbook on local church government and management. Regarding the image of military apparatus turned into agricultural tools, he writes, "The proper way to deal with conflict in the church is not through authoritative force, but through love for one another, fellowship, and support. The church is the ideal spiritual kingdom."[2] On verse 4 on God's execution of judgment, he argues that the decisions of the local church's officials who are chosen by God should be upheld.[3] He reads the language of Zion's standing out among all others as a reference to the church as superior over earthly standards. He pays particular attention to the moral and Christian character of believers in pursuing holiness and righteousness. Lastly, he understands "the establishment of Zion" as the statement of faith and the doctrinal teaching of the True Church denomination that stands strong and will not be moved by slander and false teachings.[4]

Zion as Social Justice and Peace

Another representative reading is that of Chen Nan-Chou.[5] For him, the passage is a proof text for any discussion on social justice, peace, and reconciliation. He speaks of the racial disharmony and discrimination in the world, particularly in the United States. In his commentary, he inserts an anecdote about how he was once forbidden to enter the United Nations in New York because he comes from Taiwan, not a member state. He hails Martin Luther King, with his famous "I have a dream" rhetoric, as a social activist who promoted social equality. Chen maintains that Jesus's teaching about God's kingdom and Martin Luther King's advocacy are the same. Insofar as there is a lack of peace in many parts of the world, he affirms that one can build on the work done by Martin Luther King and hope that one day there will be true justice and peace in the world. Chen's theologizing resonates well with secular and cultural justice.

---

2. 林永基《活讀以塞亞書》台中：腓利門實業股份有限公司 (Lin Yong-Ji, *Live Reading on Isaiah* [2009], 35).

3. Lin Yong-Ji, *Live Reading on Isaiah*, 35.

4. Lin Yong-Ji, 35.

5. 陳南州《上主是天上任間的主：以賽亞書 1~39章》台南:台灣教會報社 (Chen Nan-Zhou, *The Lord Is the Lord in Heaven: Isaiah 1–38* [2016]).

Ideal Zion as New Jerusalem

Jeffrey Lu reads the text in relation to Isaiah 65–66 on the vision of the New Jerusalem. This New Jerusalem is the center of international pilgrimage, revelation, and peace. He maintains that the vision speaks of the "Ideal Zion," and that the Ideal Zion is a symbol that goes beyond the historical eighth-century BCE Judah and Jerusalem but is *replaced by* the spiritual Zion. The thrice-repeated references to "Jacob" (2:3, 5, 6) and the mention of "Israel" (4:2) are seen as markers that the vision goes beyond geographical Zion.[6] This highlights the spiritual people of God in an Ideal Zion. Quoting 2 Timothy 2:22, he states that the spiritual people of God will be characterized by waiting upon God's sovereignty, seeking after God's instructions, upholding God's justice and peace, and pursuing spiritual communities that pray with a pure heart.[7]

Taiwanese Judeophilia Eschatology

Aside from the above interpretive traditions, Jewish-centered eschatology is the order of the day. The following elements characterize Taiwanese Judeophilia Eschatology (henceforth TJE).

Literal Fulfillment Eschatology

TJE is unapologetic that literal reading is the first interpretive principle unless the text before and after suggests otherwise. It argues for a literal reading by rhetorically asking: "Don't the prophecies about the Messiah have to be literally interpreted and literally fulfilled in Jesus Christ? Why then do we not interpret the prophecies about the restoration of Israel literally as well?"[8] Its hermeneutics build on the prophecies about the Messiah which were literally interpreted and fulfilled in the person of Jesus Christ.

---

6. Jeffrey Shao Chang Lu, *Isaiah* (1), Tien Dao Bible Commentary [以賽亞（Ⅰ）] (Hong Kong: Tien Dao, 2015), 138.

7. Lu, *Isaiah*, 139.

8. 「以色列復國是否應驗聖經預言？（二)」 ("Is Israel's National Restoration a Biblical Fulfilment? [Part II])," http://www.fundamentalbook.com/article193.html.

Greater attention is placed on foretelling than on forthtelling. The fulfillment of the prophecy is the centerpiece. TJE reads the promises of Isaiah 2:1–5 as first fulfilled in 1948 when Israel gained its independence led by Jewish leader and Prime Minister David Ben-Gurion. The establishment of the modern State of Israel in Palestine is considered the "watershed in human history."[9] TJE recognizes that through numerous waves of Aliyah Zionist immigration Israel will continue to return to their land and await its complete fulfillment.[10] Denny Ma associates Isaiah 2:1–5 with BYLU (*Beit Ya'akov Lekhu Ve-nelkha* [House, Jacob, Come, Walk]). This is an organization founded in 1882 that seeks to establish the restoration of Israel based on this Isaiah passage.[11]

TJE argues that God's plan for Israel was to first gather them back to their land and then give them a new circumcised heart and spirit (Ezek 11:18–20).[12] This responds to critics who question the 1948 event as the fulfillment of the prophecies and the lack of differentiation between political and spiritual Israel. Critics prioritize Jewish spiritual repentance, but, for TJE, spiritual restoration is not enough. The national restoration of Israel is also necessary.

Proponents of TJE claim that their interpretation and theology is based on the grace, wisdom, sovereignty, and faithfulness of God. "Israel's historical experience has never been experienced by other people groups and nations in the world. They have been colonized by many great and gentile nations, like Egypt, Assyria, Babylon, Persia, Romans, and Ottoman Empire, etc. but they still survive."[13] Israel's survival is a demonstration that God has a distinct plan for them. TJE cites biblical texts that include non-Jews and pagan gentiles, yet the sovereign God fulfills his plan for the Jews (e.g., through King Cyrus).

Instead of debating historical-critical issues, the TJE hermeneutical lens looks at the unfolding fulfillment of these prophecies in contemporary modern history: the current geopolitical situation in the news on the one hand, and the prophecies in the Old Testament on the

9. Timothy Lee, 「世界局勢分水嶺：以色列復國」 ("The Watershed in Human History: Israel's National Restoration") *TruthLoveShare* (blog), May 2010, http://www.luke54.org/view/18/726.html.

10. "Is Israel's National Restoration a Biblical Fulfilment? (Part II)."

11. Denny Ma, *Glory of Redemption: A Commentary on the Book of Isaiah* (Taipei: Tianen, 2005).

12. "Is Israel's National Restoration a Biblical Fulfilment? (Part II)."

13. "Is Israel's National Restoration a Biblical Fulfilment? (Part II)."

other hand.[14] Prophecy as a spiritual gift and phenomenon is a lived reality. The national and social developments of the Jews are seen as God at work rather than simply historical events of political, social, and economic causality. Since the ancient prophecies about Israel are currently being fulfilled, contemporary prophecies spoken by pastor-prophets are also deemed trustworthy. This grants license to practice prophecy in modern times.

Jewish-Privileged Eschatology

TJE concurs with the prevailing narrative that God has rejected Israel because of their unbelief in Jesus as the Messiah (Matt 8:11–12; Acts 13:46). But it is quick to say that God has not completely abandoned Israel (Rom 11:1–2, 25–29). The rejection of Israel as God's chosen people in human history is deemed temporary and partial. God's irrevocable intention is to restore the fortunes of Israel. TJE believes that the Jews have "sacred possession" of the land of Israel (Gen 17:8). "No other nations or countries, ancient or modern, not even USA or England or China have sacred possession of their respective lands. If there was any nation who has a sacred possession of their land, it would be Israel."[15] Peter Lu opines that "on that day, the place of the Jewish nation and Israelites will be higher than other non-jewish nations."[16] TJE argues that Replacement Theology has misunderstood the New Testament texts on unity (Eph 2:14; Rom 3:22; 10:12). Accordingly, unity in the church does not mean that the gentiles have replaced the Jews in God's salvation history.

Rev Nathaniel Chou argues that Replacement Theology has "suppressed" (*fēngshā*) the Jews from the "whole bowl of salvation," leaving the Jews without any share in this salvation. He preaches, "Thank God, as we are transformed, God has revealed his will to us to pay attention to our 'Jewish big brother.' We have to learn from them, love them and honor them. May God lead not only Taiwan but Chinese churches

---

14. For example, the article "Proving Biblical Prophecies: Israel Media," *Kingdom Revival Times* 738 (16 Oct. 2016), is in consonance with Pesher reading of OT texts mindful of the two horizons.

15. "Is Israel's National Restoration a Biblical Fulfilment? (Part II)."

16. Peter C. S. Lu, *A Commentary on the Book of Isaiah in the 21st Century* (Vista, CA: Christ-Centered Gospel Mission, 2004), 40.

and non-Chinese churches not to 'suppress the Jews' anymore. In the fullness of time, we will see all Jews saved."[17]

Missional Eschatology

While others read Isaiah 2:1–5 in theological abstraction and ethical–moral reflection, TJE is oriented toward evangelism and world missions. This way of reading calls the Chinese churches to participate in the evangelization of the Jews. Chinese Christians are viewed as transformative agents. Hence, long- and short-term missions teams are sent to modern Israel. Jewish missions receives more funding than that for other people groups (e.g., Muslims). Prayer rallies for Jews to believe in the Messiah Jesus Christ are on the rise. Proponents self-designate as "watchmen for Israel" (Hab 2:1). Sharing the gospel with Jews is viewed as their divine calling and a chance "to pay the debt of the gospel." Having been recipients of Western missionary work in the past, they are now self-commissioned to take the gospel back to the Jews – hence the "Back to Jerusalem" Movement as a missionary phenomenon and vision of the churches in China. They see themselves on the frontline in taking on the missionary responsibility of taking the gospel west and south of China, including the Middle East. They believe that this missionary work is a precondition for Jesus's return and will hasten it (Matt 24:14).[18]

Analogical Eschatology

Judeophilia eschatology perceives Jewish restoration as a precondition to Taiwan's national and spiritual renewal. In the vision statement of

---

17. 李容珍與林鈺庭, 「國家祭壇: 回轉到神面前得地為業」 (Nathaniel Chou, "National Prayer Altar: Return to God; Land as Inheritance") in *Chinese Christian Tribune* 3851 (Oct. 2016): 5, https://www.ct.org.tw/1295078. Rev Chou spoke about the theme of suppression (*fēngshā* 封殺): how the church in the past suppressed the Jews, Taiwan aborigines, the Jewish festivals, and the Holy Spirit, exhorting Taiwan churches to repent.

18. Paul Hattaway, *Back to Jerusalem: Three Chinese House Church Leaders Share Their Vision to Complete the Great Commission* (Carlisle: Piquant, 2003), 20.

Tabernacle of David (TOD), the goal is to pursue, first, the revival of national Israel and, second, the revival of the churches of Taiwan.[19]

Moreover, the relationship between Israel and the church is expressed not solely in terms of historical priority but also in essence. Chang explains that "whenever we talk about the election of God's people, it includes Israel as the sand of the seashore and the church as the stars in the sky; all are Abraham's descendants, natural and spiritual descendants. But the spiritual cannot come first; instead, the natural should come first (I Cor 15:46)."[20] In another sermon, he said: "God has used the restoration of Israel as the sign of God's renewal [of the world]; God will also use the church, his spiritual children, to do the work of renewal."[21] Chou identifies Israel as the "big brother" (*Zhăngzǐ*) of the church. It is believed that the revival of Taiwan as a nation is connected with the revival of Israel.

The connection is demonstrated by restoring and employing Old Testament language and themes in the local churches: blowing rams' horns, the use of the language of "altar" (*iitán*), hoisting Jewish flags, wearing Jewish clothing, celebrating the Jewish feasts and festivals, adopting the Jewish calendar, pitching tents to celebrate Sukkoth, and learning Jewish education and economics.[22] TJE rationalizes that if Taiwanese churches find their roots in the Jewish faith, they also will be recipients of God's blessings like Israel.

Contrary to Marcionism, TJE takes the Old Testament to be the authoritative revelation of God. It regards the election of Israel, their history, and culture as God's revelation to humanity rather than sim-

19. A Christian organization that publishes books, writes and produces music, organizes leadership training, etc. "We believe that before the coming of the Lord, there will be a global revival . . . Such revival at least covers four areas: (1) the revival of Israel; (2) the revival of the glorious church (spiritual Israel); (3) the revival of every tribe, every people and every nation; (4) the revival of all heaven and earth (Rom 8:18, 21). In the Bible we see the last wave of revival before the 2nd coming of the Christ; the most important movement of revival is restoring the Tabernacle of David." Accessed 11 February 2019, http://www.hosanna-tod.com/about_us/?parent_id=30.

20. 章啟明 (Chang Tzi-Min) 「從以色列的復興認識先見創意文化」 ("Discover the Creative Culture from the Revival of Israel"), August 2017, accessed 11 February 2019, http://www.hosanna-tod.com/festival/?parent_id=1643.

21. Chang, "Discover the Creative Culture from the Revival of Israel." On this website is a table which compares the restoration of Israel on the one hand with the renewal of the church.

22. The philosemitism is selective as it does not adopt the Jewish dietary system.

ply a medium of God's revelation of his salvation plan. Accordingly, Israel does not just prefigure the church. The concern for the Israel/ Jewish calendar, customs, and practices does not serve as background for understanding Old Testament texts. Instead, this approach makes the Jewish calendar and culture part of God's revelation itself.

The Rationale for the Taiwanese Judeophilia Eschatology

One's social and cultural milieu and experience affect one's interpretive strategies and theology. Despite the linguistic, geographical, cultural, and geopolitical distance between Taiwan and Israel, Taiwanese Christians have a magnetic affinity for Israel. I suggest the following three possible social and cultural realities which serve as hermeneutical contexts behind the theology.

First, geopolitically, the Taiwanese perceive themselves as the underdogs or victims of strong oppressive powers. Despite possessing a democratic government, flag, and monetary system, Taiwan is hardpressed as an independent sovereign country. The tense relationship between Taiwan and China goes back to 1949. China has moved the international community, including the UN, to withhold Taiwan independence from China.[23] Because of this kind of geopolitical humiliation, in addition to the history of Western colonization and the context of a shame culture, Taiwan identifies with the Jews whose geopolitical sovereignty is also constantly under threat. The Old Testament language of "possessing the land as heritage," "restoration/renewal of the land," and "freedom from bondage" appeals to TJE and is part of their corporate prayers.

Second, although the Taiwanese are steeped in shamanism and ancestral worship, Taiwan is increasingly a secular and materialistic society. The Taiwanese are more interested in economics than politics.[24] Neighboring the larger economic market of China, the Taiwanese are

23. Ng Yuzin Chiautong, 「台灣與中國關係的探索」 ("An Excursion into the Relationships between Taiwan and China") in 臺灣國際研究季刊 8, no. 1 (2012): 1–12; Jeanne Hoffman, "Taiwan Trap: New Stories Needed – Rethinking Taiwan and China Futures," *Journal of Future Studies* 21, no. 4 (2017): 1–17; Sui-Sheng Jao, "Chinese Nationalism and Beijing's Taiwan Policy: A China Threat?," *Issues & Studies* 36, no. 1 (2000): 76–99.

24. Chun-Chi Chang and Te-Sheng Chen, "Idealism versus Reality: An Empirical Test of Postmaterialism in China and Taiwan," in *Issues & Studies* 49, no. 2 (2013): 63–102.

looking for new paradigms to achieve economic and financial prosperity.[25] In the eyes of the Taiwanese, the Jews are known to be rich, famous, and successful.[26] The Chinese psyche wants to emulate the best practices and practitioners of economic prosperity. This explains the preponderance of Jewish economic management books in the Taiwanese market.[27] Given the combination of the seduction of the prosperity gospel, the force of materialism, and the economic growth and development of Mainland China, it is not surprising that this kind of Judeophilia strikes a chord with many Taiwanese Christians.[28]

Third, Taiwanese culture is grounded in the teachings of Confucianism and Taoism. As a social and ethical philosophy,[29] Confucianism accounts for the personal, social, and environmental realms of human existence. Insofar as the Jewish culture has deep moral and ethical traditions regarding family, education, and lifestyle, Taiwanese Christians have a strong affinity for it.[30] Books on Jewish child education translated into Chinese are available in local bookstores.[31] Taiwanese Bible-reading practices focus on the moral teachings rather than on the doctrinal, historical, or political aspects of the Old Testament.

25. Shin-Ta Tung, "Economics and Business of Great China from Taiwan's Perspective," 創新與管理 12, no. 3 (2016): 73–94.

26. In the 2017 Forbes World's Billionaires list, five Jews were in the top 15 and seven in the top 25. Mark Zuckerberg is the world's richest Jew. Wang Jianlin from China ranked 18 and Li Ka-Sheng ranked 19.

27. Rabbi Daniel Lapin's *Thou Shall Prosper* was translated into Chinese (猶太人致富金律) in 2009. A book by Zvika Bergman entitled *Secrets the Rich Jews Know* was translated into Chinese in 2015.

28. James Ross and Song Lihong, *The Image of Jews in Contemporary China* (Boston: Academic Studies Press, 2016). Lihong maintains that in China, the fascination for Jewish/Israeli culture is mainly economic and educational, without the religious aspect, unlike in Taiwan. Lihong Song, "Some Observations on Chinese Jewish Studies," *Contemporary Jewry* 29 (2009): 195–214. DOI: 10.1007/s12397-009-9016-9.

29. Kwok Pui-Lan, "Chinese Christians and Their Bible," *Biblical Interpretation* 4, no. 1 (1996): 127–129. Confucianism is not a religion for it has little to say about metaphysical and spiritual realities. Should there be any metaphysical reality, it is more an abstract concept than a person.

30. Der-Heuy Yee, 「台灣本地行事邏輯的探討：尋找尚未接上的環節」 ("Social Betterment in the Realm of Practical Ethics in Taiwanese Society: In Search of a Missing Link"), 慈濟大學人文社會科學學刊 7 (2008): 25–63.

31. For example, Wendy Mogel, *The Blessing of a Skinned Knee: Using Jewish Teachings to Raise Self-Reliant Children* (孩子需要9種福分：古猶太教的教養智慧) (Scribner, 2008); Sara Imas, *Jewish Mother Gives Three Keys to Children: Viability, Will Power, Ability to Solve Problems* (猶太媽媽給孩子的3把金鑰：生存力、意志力、解決問題的能力) (2015).

In sum, the observation of Philip Jenkins that the Global South is characterized by "its veneration for Old Testament, which is considered as authoritative as the New"[32] is now confirmed. Taiwanese culture has more similarities with Jewish than with Western and Greek cultures. Regarding the Jews as the "big brother" of the church resonates well since ancestral and family solidarity, and respect for the elderly and one's predecessors are intrinsic aspects of the culture.

Toward a Taiwanese Eschatological *Ta-Tung* Reading of Isaiah 2:1–5

The prophet Isaiah's vision in Isaiah 2:1–5 of communal peace and harmony is attractive to Taiwanese culture. The concept of harmony is composed of two Chinese characters 大同, *Ta-Tung*. *Ta-Tung* is an ideology that has reached the popular level as an everyday motto among Taiwanese. It is used to designate major thoroughfares, businesses, edifices, hotels, and educational institutions; and, most importantly, *Ta-Tung* appears among the lyrics of the Taiwan National Anthem. Sun Yat-Sen wrote this anthem to instill among the citizens the pursuit of *Ta-Tung*, translated here as "world peace":

> Three Principles of the People,
> Our aim shall be:
> To found a free land,
> World peace, be our stand.
> Lead on, comrades,
> Vanguards ye are. . . .
> Be earnest and brave,
> Your country to save,
> One heart, one soul,
> One mind, one goal . . .[33]

Confucius once wrote a poem to describe his *Ta-Tung* commonwealth vision:

---

32. Philip Jenkins, *The New Faces of Christianity: Believing the Bible in the Global South* (Oxford: Oxford University Press, 2006), 4–5.

33. https://en.wikipedia.org/wiki/National_Anthem_of_the_Republic_of_China.

When the Great Principle prevails, the world is a Commonwealth in which rulers are selected according to their wisdom and ability. Mutual confidence is promoted and good neighborliness cultivated. Hence, men do not regard as parents only their own parents, nor do they treat as children only their own children. Provision is secured for the aged till death, employment for the able-bodied, and the means of growing up for the young. Helpless widows and widowers, orphans and the lonely, as well as the sick and the disabled, are well cared for. Men have their respective occupations and women their homes. They do not like to see wealth lying idle, yet they do not keep it for their own gratification. They despise indolence, yet they do not use their energies for their own benefit. In this way, selfish schemings are repressed, and robbers, thieves and other lawless men no longer exist, and there is no need for people to shut their doors. This is called the Great Harmony (*Ta-Tung*). [English translation by James Legge]

Kang Yu-Wei (19 March 1858 – 31 March 1927) captured this utopian vision and developed it further by setting out concrete methods and procedures to achieve it. As a political thinker and reformer of the late Qing dynasty, he wrote the book *Ta-Tung Shu* (The Book of the Great Harmony).

Kang mulls over an alternative to Buddhism's solution to the problem of human suffering. Buddhism's way to overcome suffering is to make human desire extinct – to suppress desire in any way possible. Kang, however, proposes an alternative narrative, speaking strongly about "The Evils of Having Sovereign States." Sovereign states cause different types of human suffering like war, violence, and bloodshed. He writes:

Coming now to the [matter of] existence of states, then there is quarrelling of the land, quarrelling over cities, and the people are trained to be soldiers. In a single war those who die [will number in] the thousands and ten thousands. [They] may meet with arrows, stones, lances, cannon, poison gas. And then again, [they] may be disemboweled or decapitated, [their] blood splashed on the field, [their] limbs hung in the trees. Sometimes they are thrown into a river, dragging each other under. Sometimes a whole city is burned. Sometimes the corpses are strewn everywhere and dogs fight over them. Sometimes half [of the army] lies wounded, and then hunger and pestilence continue the deaths.[34]

His political strategy to achieve sustainable peace and harmony is two-fold: complete military disarmament and the abolition of sovereign boundaries. The way he expresses this is powerful: "The desire to bring about peace among men cannot [be accomplished] without disarmament; and the desire to bring about disarmament cannot [be accomplished] without abolishing sovereign states."[35]

He proposes the abolition of nine boundaries which will lead to harmony in the One World:

1. Abolishing National Boundaries and Uniting the World
2. Abolishing Class Boundaries and Equalizing [All] People
3. Abolishing Racial Boundaries and Amalgamating the Races
4. Abolishing Sex Boundaries and Preserving Independence
5. Abolishing Family Boundaries and Becoming "Heaven's People"
6. Abolishing Livelihood Boundaries and Making Occupations Public
7. Abolishing Administrative Boundaries and Governing with Complete Peace-and-Equality
8. Abolishing Boundaries of Kind, and Loving All Living [Things]
9. Abolishing Boundaries of Suffering and Attaining Utmost Happiness

Finally, a student of Confucius's Three-Age paradigm, he envisages that this One World will be the product of evolution in three stages:[36]

First Stage: The Age of Disorder at the Time the First Foundations of One World Is Laid
Second Stage: The Age of Increasing Peace-and-Equality When One World Is Gradually Coming into Being
Third Stage: The Age of Complete Peace-and-Equality When One World Has Been Achieved

34. Kang, Yu-Wei, *Ta t'ung shu: The One-World Philosophy of Kang Yu-Wei*, trans. and Introduction by Laurence G. Thompson (London: George Allen & Unwin, 1958), 81.
35. Kang, *Ta t'ung shu*, 83.
36. Kang, 72.

To be sure, Kang's *Ta-Tung* vision cannot be indiscriminately adopted as Christian eschatology. In fact, Kang could be censured as naïve, a racist, a polygamist, and an atheist according to modern and Christian sensibilities given his views on humanity, race, and marriage. For instance, there is naïveté in supposing that human beings will naturally and progressively become good in the final stage. His racism is observable when he says: "when the One World is attained, there will remain only the white and yellow race. The black and brown race will probably all be swept away from the earth."[37] He is guilty of promoting polygamy, believing that monogamy goes against human nature and desire.[38] Assuredly, Kang's utopian vision falls short of the Christian vision of eschatology. His *Ta-Tung* lacks Christian theistic foundations. Most importantly, a day of judgment is not in his purview. He writes:

> Christianity takes reverence for God and love for men as a teaching of the Good; it takes repentance of sin and judgment after death as its [means of making people] frightened by [doing] evil. In the Age of Complete Peace-and-Equality, [people] will naturally love others, will naturally be without sin. Comprehending the natural workings of evolution, they will therefore not reverence God. Comprehending the impossibility [literally, "difficulty"] of limitless numbers of souls occupying the space [of Heaven], they therefore will not believe in a Day of Judgement. The religion of Jesus therefore, when we have attained One World, will be extinct.[39]

Kang's *Ta-Tung* vision certainly lacks a Christian orientation, but as a nonbiblical text his idea should not be quickly dismissed. Instead, his views may be conceived as a collaborative witness to crucial aspects of Christian and biblical eschatology. They are instructive for theological reflection and provide a guide map for Christian eschatology. Thus, the following discussion is a reappropriation of Kang's concept of *Ta-Tung* infused with christological and ecclesiological underpinnings.

37. Kang, 274–275.
38. Kang, 63.
39. Kang, 274–275.

From National Self-Determination to One Administration under Jesus Christ

Kang's problematization of sovereign states and boundaries is the crux in any serious discussion of world peace and human equality. Insofar as sovereign statehood leads to endless war and violence, Kang is unafraid to call out national sovereignty as the elephant in the room in any peace talks. He writes: "Even the Good and Upright cannot help but be partial each to his own state. Hence, what their wills are fixed upon, what they know and talk about, is always limited to [their own] state. [They] consider fighting for territory and killing other people to be an important duty; they consider destroying other states and butchering their people to be a great accomplishment."[40] Kang also rightly observes: "nowadays disarmament conferences are being held ever more frequently, and such [conferences] aside, whenever individual states make treaties, these treaties are always based upon the principle of disarmament. Nevertheless, so long as the boundaries of states are not abolished, and the strong and the weak, the large and the small are mixed in together, wishing to plan for disarmament is [like] ordering tigers and wolves to be vegetarians – it must fail."[41]

Kang's proposal of disarmament may be provocative in modern society, but it is nevertheless in line with the language of demilitarization in Isaiah 2:4, "they shall beat their swords into plowshares, and their spears into pruning hooks; nation shall not lift up sword against nation, neither shall they learn war any more." He further proposes that in the One World, nationalism will be abolished and everyone will be under one administration. He writes: "In the Age of One World there will be no national struggles, no secret schemes. In great undertakings it will not be necessary to put power into the hands of political leaders or set up autocratic leaders. The laws and regulations of the ten thousand and some hundred administrative [organs] will all be [determined] through universal public discussion."[42]

The Isaiah passage envisions all nations making pilgrimage to Zion as the dwelling place of God (the temple). Although the vision is prefaced and directed to Judah and Jerusalem (v. 1), the objective is internationalism. The picture does not encourage hegemonic power or

40. Kang, 82.
41. Kang, 83.
42. Kang, 235.

the superiority of one nation over another. Instead, the Lord rules and arbitrates among these nations. The focus of TJE unwittingly shifts from awaiting the second coming of Christ to awaiting the eschatological restoration of Israel. While TJE claims that its vision is Christ-centered, its eschatology does not fully exhaust the role of Jesus Christ and the church as the final and perfect revelation of God. Jesus and the church are the ultimate realities prefigured in the Old Testament Law, Prophets, and Writings (Heb 10:1). N. T. Wright argues that a christological reading of the restoration of Israel in Old Testament eschatological passages leads one to view God's promises in the Old Testament as all fulfilled in Jesus Christ. In Christ every one of God's promises is a "Yes." For this reason it is through Jesus that we say "Amen," to the glory of God. Jesus's resurrection is the fulfillment of the restoration of the temple. Jesus's redemptive work of the whole world fulfills the promise of restoration of the land. N. T. Wright says poignantly:

> The NT is unequivocal in its interpretation of the fall of Jerusalem as being inextricably linked to the vindication of Jesus and his people. Jesus' whole claim is to do and be what the city and the temple were and did. Any attempt to claim that they can (on the basis of a supposed "literal" meaning of the many Old Testament promises of restoration, as yet supposedly unfulfilled) has failed to reckon with the total New Testament reading of those promises . . . they all have come true in the Messiah (2 Cor. 1:20). This is no simple spiritualization. Rather, these promises, seen now through the lens of the cross and the resurrection, have been in one sense narrowed down to a point and in another sense widened to include the whole created order.[43]

Kang's proposition regarding public discussion on policies may be strategic – in fact, it is very modern and humanistic. This humanism results in the lack of divine administrator in his vision. The biblical vision introduces Jesus Christ as God – the one ushering in the kingdom of God. He reigns as King and Lord over his people. It is this rule that will abrogate the sovereignty of states and self-determination. It will effect the leveling of all nations and the prioritizing of communal life.

---

43. N. T. Wright, "Jerusalem in the New Testament," in *Jerusalem Past and Present in the Purposes of God*, ed. P. W. L. Walker (Grand Rapids: Baker; Carlisle: Paternoster, 1994), 53–77, here 73.

More importantly, Kang is laudable in singling out selfishness as the moral–ethical thrust of the matter. After all, is not "national interest" the operative word we hear in any geopolitical discussion? He incisively writes that "cultivating the spirit of aggressiveness and selfishness, [men] are led to rationalize and justify their narrow-mindedness and cruelty."[44] Make no mistake, selflessness is antithetical to sovereignty, self-determination, and national interest.

Selflessness is the central message of Jesus Christ in his teaching and also in his work at the cross. After all, he sacrificially gave himself up for human beings to rescue them (Gal 1:4; 1 Tim 2:6). Self-denial and selflessness for the sake of others is required of the church of Christ as the people of God in Philippians 2:3–4 ("Do nothing from selfish ambition or conceit, but in humility regard others as better than yourselves. Let each of you look not to your own interests, but to the interests of others"). The New Testament is replete with texts on the people of God maintaining love and peace (1 Cor 13:13; Eph 2:1–17; 4:2; Col 3:12–14).

From Geographical Attachment to the Whole Earth for Everyone

Kang seeks to abolish sovereign states based on geography. He maintains that "In One World there will be no need to attach importance to geographical factors . . . there being no states or military strong points."[45] The whole earth will be divided for everyone. "In the One World, transportation, communication and settlement of population will open up the whole earth, so that there will no longer be any isolated or backward areas."[46] He adds, "In the Age of One World, the [peoples] of the whole earth will all be self-governing, and the whole earth will be entirely under one great administration, publicly elected by the people."[47]

Similarly, it is unnecessary to be fixated on the sanctity of geographical Jerusalem. Israel's land, election, institutions, and culture should be understood as instruments of God's revelation. Without them, God's revelation would have had no way to reach human beings. Christopher Wright says aptly:

44. Kang, *Ta t'ung shu*, 82.
45. Kang, 231.
46. Kang, 231.
47. Kang, 232.

When prophets spoke about the future, they could only do so mean-ingfully by using terms and realities that existed in their past or present experience. The realities associated with being Israel in their day included their specific history and such things as the land, the law, Jerusalem, the temple, sacrifices and priesthood. All of these had substantial significance in Israel's relationship with God, and also in Israel's ultimate role in relation to the nations . . . Thus, for prophets to speak about God's future dealings with Israel and the nations, they had to speak in terms of these contemporary realities.[48]

Wright maintains that there is a transcendent nature to the prophe-cies as well, such that they go beyond Israel's historical nationhood. He writes: "Moreover, even in the Old Testament itself, there was an awareness that the fulfillment of prophecies that were made in terms of the concrete realities of Israel's life and faith would actually go beyond them. The familiar dimensions of Israel's national life are transcended in various ways."[49]

God's sacred space, historically located in Jerusalem, is now ex-panded to cover the world as the knowledge of God fills the whole earth ("But the earth will be filled with the knowledge of the glory of the Lord, as the waters cover the sea" Hab 2:14). Jerusalem is merely a microcosm of God's dwelling place that is the whole earth. Taiwanese Christians' impassioned interest in mission work by going to remote places to bear witness to the knowledge and glory of God should be understood as a theological act. The sacred space has been redefined to include all parts of the world where God's glory is manifest. "If there are 'holy places' in the land for Christians to visit, they must be regarded, in some senses, as one might regard the grave of a dearly loved friend, perhaps even an older brother."[50]

Kang's concept of whole-earth *Ta-Tung* finds parallels in the biblical vision of the kingdom of God introduced by Jesus Christ. It does not place a high premium on one geographical region over another. N. T. Wright criticizes Judeophilia eschatology since it undermines what Jesus has accomplished:

48. Christopher Wright, "A Christian Approach to Old Testament Prophecy con-cerning Israel," in Walker, *Jerusalem Past and Present*, 3.

49. C. Wright, "Christian Approach," 4.

50. N. T. Wright, "Jerusalem in the New Testament," 76.

The attempt to carry over some OT promises about Jerusalem, the land and the temple for fulfilment in our own day has the same theological shape as the attempt in pre-Reformation Catholicism to think of Christ as being re-crucified in every Mass . . . If Jesus was claiming to be, in effect, the new and true temple, and his death is to be seen as the drawing together into one of the history of Israel in her desolation, dying her death outside the walls of the city, and rising again as the beginning of the real "restoration," the real return from exile, then the attempt to say that there are some parts of the Old Testament (relating to Jerusalem, Land or Temple) which have not yet been "fulfilled" and so need a historical and literal "fulfilment" now, or at some other time, is an explicit attempt to take something away from the achievement of Christ in his death and resurrection, and to preserve it for the work of human beings in a different time and place. The work of Christ is . . . "incomplete."[51]

From Racial/Class Privileging to Equalizing All People

Kang's discussion on the abolition of racial and class boundaries, while ideal, is naïve and problematic. Although the intention is to abolish the boundaries, his methodology may be faulted as racism for privileging white and yellow skin color over brown and black: "The silver-colored race is spread out over the globe, while the gold-colored race is still more numerous. These two kinds – the yellow and the white – have occupied the whole world. The strength of the white race is assuredly superior, while the yellow race is more numerous and also wise. But it is an indestructible principle that when [two kinds] join in union they are smelted."[52]

Kang is cognizant that this boundary is the most difficult one to abolish. His method is problematic (racist and sexist) as he proposes mixed marriage, interracial propagation, the non-white race practice of migration, and a change of diet to change skin color. When it comes to social classes, he identifies three inferior classes: the inferior race, slaves, and women. For all three, he provides a masterplan to abolish these boundaries. Kang's method of achieving the uniformity of color is ludicrous, but the intention to abolish racial discrimination needs

51. N. T. Wright, 73–74.
52. Kang, *Ta t'ung shu*, 141.

a biblical assessment. This is a necessary corrective to a highly Jewish-centered eschatology.

Taiwanese eschatology would do better to embrace the apostle Paul's message: "For in Christ Jesus you are all children of God through faith. As many of you as were baptized into Christ have clothed yourselves with Christ. There is no longer Jew or Greek, there is no longer slave or free, there is no longer male and female; for all of you are one in Christ Jesus. And if you belong to Christ, then you are Abraham's offspring, heirs according to the promise" (Gal 3:26–29). Certainly, this passage is not about non-differentiation, but affirms the peace, unity, and equality between the two people groups. It imagines a world where Jews and gentiles (Taiwanese Christians) are equal. Discrimination of other races (antisemitism) and privileging the Jewish race and culture (philosemitism) over others and, even worse, over one's own culture should be denounced. TJE's Judeophilia is a disservice to Taiwanese Christianity. The recognition by gentile Christians of Jews as "big brothers" should be redefined as simply respecting Jewish status as that of the firstborn and those who have historical priority without ascribing them superiority over other people groups. The relationship could be conceived as that of twin brothers rather than as an older-and-younger brother relationship.

Using a Christ-centered ecclesiological lens when reading the Old Testament prophecies will highlight the equal place of Jews and gentiles in God's redemptive plan in and through Jesus Christ. Also, an ecclesiological lens will reframe the reading from a Jewish-centered one to a universal one, and affirm the diversity of the church as the people of God. Every race/color is a member of the body and contributes to the universal nature of the church. Abolishing differences of race/color is unbiblical (Rev 7:9–10).

From War and Violence to Productivity and Benevolence

Kang supposes that when all the racial, gender, social, and national boundaries have been removed, placing everyone on the same plane, humanity will finally have reached the Third Stage of One World. In that One World, the world will not be stagnant. The competition arising from acting in selfishness and national interests present in the first stage will be transformed. The people of One World will compete in (1) the pursuit of excellence, (2) the pursuit of knowledge, and (3) encouraging *jen* (human benevolence). All three are simply different aspects of the same method: to rechannel the competitive drive of humanity into a constructive form of competition. There will be no military, economic, political, or social competition, but people will compete to produce the best material goods, to invent new methods, to expand knowledge, and to manifest their *jen* (human benevolence). Through this cooperative kind of competition the world will not fear the stagnation of civilization or retrogression into the disorderly stage, but will continue to progress.[53]

Kang operates within the context of secular and humanistic benevolence (*jen*), but if this *jen* is redeemed from its secular context and reoriented toward Christ and the church, the pursuit of *jen* becomes the "responsibility of the church in the present to anticipate the age to come in acts of justice, mercy, beauty and truth; we are to live 'now' as it will be 'then.' We can only do this . . . there is no going back to the old lines that demarcate human beings (race, color, gender, geography)."[54] If in the One World "people will honour virtue and not nobility of [blood],"[55] then in the kingdom of Jesus Christ people will live the life of the Beatitudes as the light and salt of the world (Matt 5:13–16). This pursuit of moral virtue rather than power politics is consistent with Isaiah when he imagines the adherence to the Torah of the Lord coming out of Zion.

Closing Remarks

Similar to many other human-centered visions of utopia, another significant weakness of Kang's *Ta-Tung* narrative is its temporal and earthly scope. His *Ta-Tung* is confined to human earthly life. Recognizing the inevitability of human ageing and death, Kang can only outline measures to prevent sickness and death in the Age of Complete Peace and Equality in the One World. He presses for a vegetarian diet, cultivation of a healthy environment, effective medical support, facilities to prolong human life, and also the study of Buddhahood and immortality. On the last point on Buddhahood, he is at his wits' end, saying:

53. Kang, 49–50.
54. N. T. Wright, "Jerusalem in the New Testament," 76; cf. a constructive view of *jen* in K. K. Yeo, *Musing with Confucius and Paul: Toward a Chinese Christian Theology* (Eugene: Cascade, 2008), 253–354.
55. Kang, 245.

The One World is the ultimate Law of this world; but the study of immortality, of longevity without death, is even an extension of the ultimate Law of this world. The study of Buddhahood . . . [implies] not [merely] a setting apart from the world, but [an actual] going out of this world; still more, it is going out of the One World. If we go this far, then we abandon the human sphere and enter the sphere of immortals and Buddhas . . . the study of immortality is too crude, its subtle words and profound principles are not many, and its [ability] to intoxicate men's minds is limited.[56]

This substantial limitation accentuates the superiority and the distinctiveness of the Christian utopia. In the last lines of the Nicene Creed, those who confess Jesus Christ as Lord will inevitably face death – but they will also receive physical resurrected bodies and life. It is only in and through this resurrected body that the pursuit of wisdom and human benevolence (*jen*) in the world to come can reach its ultimate potential. These bodies will flourish in the enduring administration of Jesus Christ, without war and boundaries, and without end.

For Further Reading

Blaising, Craig, and Darrell Bock, eds. *Progressive Dispensationalism.* Grand Rapids: Baker, 2000.

Finto, Don. *God's Promise and the Future of Israel.* Ventura: Regal, 2006.

Kang, Yu-Wei. *Ta t'ung shu: The One-World Philosophy of Kang Yu-Wei.* Translation and Introduction by Laurence G. Thompson. London: George Allen & Unwin, 1958.

Lu, Jeffrey Shao Chang. *Isaiah (1).* Tien Dao Bible Commentary. Hong Kong: Tien Dao, 2015.

Ross, James, and Song Lihong. *The Image of Jews in Contemporary China.* Boston: Academic Studies Press, 2016.

Walker, P. W. L. *Jerusalem Past and Present in the Purposes of God.* 2nd ed. Carlisle: Paternoster; Grand Rapids: Baker, 1994.

Walls, Jerry L., ed. *The Oxford Handbook of Eschatology.* Oxford: Oxford University Press, 2008.

---

56. *The One-World Philosophy of Kang Yu-Wei,* 275.

Contributors

John David Kwamena Ekem (Dr Theol., *magna cum laude*, University of Hamburg) is Professor of New Testament Studies and Director, Centre for Mother Tongue Biblical Hermeneutics at Trinity Theological Seminary, Legon, Accra, Ghana. He is also the Seminary's Vice-President responsible for Academic Affairs. An ordained minister of The Methodist Church Ghana, he also occupies the Seminary's Kwesi Dickson-Gilbert Ansre Distinguished Chair of Biblical Exegesis & Mother Tongue Hermeneutics, and serves as Translation Consultant for The Bible Society of Ghana. He has supervised the translation and revision of the Bible into several major Ghanaian languages and continues to do so. A member of Studiorum Novi Testamenti Societas (Society for New Testament Studies), he has authored several books on mother-tongue biblical interpretation, including *New Testament Concepts of Atonement in an African Pluralistic Setting* (Accra: SonLife Press, 2005); *Early Scriptures of the Gold Coast (Ghana)* (Rome: Edizioni di Storia e Letteratura/Manchester: St Jerome Publishing, 2011); and, most recently, *A Simplified Greek–English Commentary on the Epistle to the Colossians* (Accra: SonLife Press, 2017), adapted from original commentaries he wrote in the Asante-Twi and Mfantse dialects of Ghana.

Shirley S. Ho (PhD, Trinity Evangelical Divinity School) is an associate professor of Old Testament at China Evangelical Seminary, Taipei, Taiwan. She is a Filipino-Chinese but has resided in Taiwan for thirteen years. Her areas of interest are Hebrew language, wisdom literature, Old Testament theology, cultural exegesis, contextual theology, and hermeneutics. She has written a number of articles, and she contributed the "Introduction and Notes on Ecclesiastes" to *NIV God's Justice Bible: The Flourishing of Creation and the Destruction of Evil*. She is a Langham Scholar and is currently doing her Langham postdoctoral research on the book of Proverbs.

James Henry Owino Kombo (PhD, Stellenbosch University) is a Kenyan Anglican minister and Professor of Theological Studies at Daystar University, Nairobi, Kenya. His outstanding publications include *The Doctrine of God in African Christian Thought* (Leiden: Brill, 2007) and *Theological Models of the Doctrine of the Trinity: The Trinity, Diversity and Theological Hermeneutics* (Carlisle, UK: Langham Global Library, 2016). Though focused on theological studies, Prof. Kombo continues to serve in the senior management of Daystar University, having been Deputy Vice-Chancellor (Academic Affairs) for ten years and acting Vice-Chancellor since November 2015. He is an active member of the Africa Society of Evangelical Theology (ASET) and editor of the *Africa Journal of Evangelical Society*.

D. Stephen Long (PhD, Duke University) is Cary M. Maguire University Professor of Ethics at Southern Methodist University, Dallas, Texas, USA. He is an ordained United Methodist minister in the Indiana Conference. He works at the intersection between theology and ethics and has published over fifty essays and fifteen books on theology and ethics, including *Divine Economy: Theology and the Market* (New York: Routledge, 2000); *The Goodness of God: Theology, Church and Social Order* (Grand Rapids: BrazosPress, 2001); *John Wesley's Moral Theology: The Quest for God and Goodness* (Wolfeboro, NH: Kingswood, 2005); *Calculated Futures* (Baylor: Baylor University Press, 2007); *Christian Ethics: A Very Short Introduction* (Oxford: OUP, 2010); *Saving Karl Barth: Hans Urs von Balthasar's Preoccupation* (Minneapolis: Fortress, 2014); *The Perfectly Simple Triune God: Aquinas and His Legacy* (Minneapolis: Fortress, 2016); and *Augustinian and Ecclesial Christian Ethics: On Loving Enemies* (Minneapolis: Fortress, 2018).

Nelson R. Morales Fredes (PhD Theological Studies/New Testament, Trinity International University) is Professor of New Testament and Hermeneutics at Seminario Teológico Centroamericano, Guatemala. Originally from Chile, he has lived, studied, and taught in Guatemala since 1993. He has written several articles in the journal *Kairós*, encyclopedia entries, a commentary on 2 Corinthians in *Comentario Bíblico Contemporáneo* (San Sebastián: Certeza Unida / Buenos Aires: Ediciones Kairós), and *Poor and Rich in James: A Relevance Theory Approach to James's Use of the Old Testament* in the Bulletin for Biblical Research Supplement Series (University Park, PA: Eisenbrauns, 2018). He is also a board member of the Evangelical Society for Socio-Religious Studies (SEES) in Guatemala.

Steve Pardue (PhD, Wheaton College) is Associate Professor of Theology at the Asia Graduate School of Theology, Manila, Philippines. He is the author of *The Mind of Christ: Humility and the Intellect in Early Christian Theology* (London/New York: Bloomsbury T&T Clark, 2012) and co-editor of *Asian Christian Theology* (Carlisle, UK: Langham Global Library). He grew up in the Philippines and moved back there after finishing his doctoral work. His areas of research include virtue theory, contextual theology, and the doctrine of providence.

Aldrin M. Peñamora (PhD Theology, Christian Ethics Concentration, Fuller Theological Seminary) is Executive Director of the Commission on Justice, Peace and Reconciliation of the Philippine Council of Evangelical Churches. He is also Executive Director of the center of Research for Christian–Muslim Relations. He has taught theology at the Koinonia Theological Seminary, Davao City, Philippines and is currently a member of the faculty of the Asian Graduate School of Theology, Philippines, and the Asian Theological Seminary, Quezon City, Philippines. As an advocate of just peace-building among different faith traditions, especially between Christians and Muslims in the Philippines and Southeast Asia, he is often involved in initiatives aimed at fostering harmonious Christian–Muslim relations. He has published essays on the subject both locally and internationally. Aldrin is married to Christine Ching Peñamora.

Alberto F. Roldán (Dr Theo., Instituto Universitario Isedet) is from Argentina. He is Postgraduate Studies Director of Instituto Teológico Fiet, Buenos Aires, Argentina, and visiting professor at Lee University, Semisud, Ecuador, South African Theological Seminary, Bryanston, South Africa, and Universidad Adventista del Plata, Libertador San Martin, Argentina. He is a prolific writer, having authored or edited thirty books, including *¿Para qué sirve la teología?* (Grand Rapids: Libros Desafío, 2011); *Reino, política y misión* (Lima: Ediciones Puma, 2011); *Atenas y Jerusalén en diálogo: Filosofía y teología en la mediación hermenéutica* (Lima: Ediciones Puma, 2015); *Hermenéutica y signos de los tiempos* (Buenos Aires: Teología y Cultura, 2016); *La teología de la cruz como crítica radical a la teología de la prosperidad*, Aportes Teológicos 3 (San José: UBL, 2018). He is a member of Fraternidad Teológica Latinoamericana (FTL) and the Society of Biblical Literature (SBL), and was awarded "Theological Personality of 2016" by the Asociación Evangélica de Educación Teológica en América Latina" (AETAL). Roldán is also the Director of Teología y Cultura: www.teologos.com.ar.

Index of Names

Index of Scripture

Old Testament

New Testament

Index of Subjects

A
African Christianity 33, 34, 37, 38, 41, 46, 48–50
Akamba 60
Aliyah Zionist 132
amillennial 51, 73
amillennialist 74
Apocalypse 18, 26, 29, 125
apocalyptic 14, 15, 18, 19, 22, 27–29, 51–53
apocalypticism 20, 27
Argentinean 78

B
Back to Jerusalem Movement (BJM) 106, 116–118, 124

C
catastrophic 15, 16, 28, 29
Choson dynasty 112
christological 87, 121, 122, 141, 143
Confucianism 107, 112, 137
cosmology 33, 37, 49, 125
cruciform eschatology 105

D
Dae-jo dong 113
de-eschatologization 1
de Gama epoch 108, 109
demigods 42
dialectical 22
Dispensationalism 73
    classic 71

progressive 71, 72
dispensationalist 16, 17, 73, 76, 77
    classic 73

E
eschatology 11, 13, 15, 16, 18, 20–22, 26, 31, 33, 34, 36, 97, 116
    analogical 134
    Asian 105, 109, 125
    cruciform 121
    dispensationalist 8
    ecocentric 66
    in song 78
    Jewish-privileged 133
    Judeophilia 134, 145
    Latin American 88
    missional 134
    Pentecostal 3, 76
    premillennial 117
    Spanish 73
eschaton 4, 11, 15, 17, 20, 22, 23, 25, 39, 70, 104
ethics 18, 20–22, 24

F
First Sino-Japanese War (1894–1895) 110
Futurist 51

G
Ghanaian 51, 60, 63, 65, 66
Ghanaian context 7, 65
Gibok Shinang 115

Langham Literature and its imprints are a ministry of Langham Partnership.

Langham Partnership is a global fellowship working in pursuit of the vision God entrusted to its founder John Stott –

> *to facilitate the growth of the church in maturity and Christ-likeness through raising the standards of biblical preaching and teaching.*

Our vision is to see churches in the majority world equipped for mission and growing to maturity in Christ through the ministry of pastors and leaders who believe, teach and live by the Word of God.

Our mission is to strengthen the ministry of the Word of God through:

- nurturing national movements for biblical preaching
- fostering the creation and distribution of evangelical literature
- enhancing evangelical theological education

especially in countries where churches are under-resourced.

Our ministry

Langham Preaching partners with national leaders to nurture indigenous biblical preaching movements for pastors and lay preachers all around the world. With the support of a team of trainers from many countries, a multi-level programme of seminars provides practical training, and is followed by a programme for training local facilitators. Local preachers' groups and national and regional networks ensure continuity and ongoing development, seeking to build vigorous movements committed to Bible exposition.

Langham Literature provides majority world preachers, scholars and seminary libraries with evangelical books and electronic resources through publishing and distribution, grants and discounts. The programme also fosters the creation of indigenous evangelical books in many languages, through writer's grants, strengthening local evangelical publishing houses, and investment in major regional literature projects, such as one volume Bible commentaries like *The Africa Bible Commentary* and *The South Asia Bible Commentary*.

Langham Scholars provides financial support for evangelical doctoral students from the majority world so that, when they return home, they may train pastors and other Christian leaders with sound, biblical and theological teaching. This programme equips those who equip others. Langham Scholars also works in partnership with majority world seminaries in strengthening evangelical theological education. A growing number of Langham Scholars study in high quality doctoral programmes in the majority world itself. As well as teaching the next generation of pastors, graduated Langham Scholars exercise significant influence through their writing and leadership.

To learn more about Langham Partnership and the work we do visit **langham.org**